Robert Holmes

On the prophecies and testimony of John the Baptist

Robert Holmes

On the prophecies and testimony of John the Baptist

ISBN/EAN: 9783337113704

Printed in Europe, USA, Canada, Australia, Japan

Cover: Foto ©Lupo / pixelio.de

More available books at **www.hansebooks.com**

On the Prophecies and Testimony of John the Baptist, and the parallel Prophecies of Jesus Christ,

EIGHT SERMONS

PREACHED BEFORE THE

UNIVERSITY OF OXFORD,

IN THE YEAR 1782,

AT THE LECTURE FOUNDED BY THE

REV. JOHN BAMPTON, M. A.
LATE CANON OF SALISBURY.

BY ROBERT HOLMES, M. A.
FELLOW OF NEW-COLLEGE.

OXFORD.

PRINTED FOR D. PRINCE AND J. COOKE, AND J. F. AND
C. RIVINGTON, AND T. CADELL, LONDON.
M DCC LXXX II.

Imprimatur,

SAM. DENNIS.

Vice-Can. OXON.

June 19. 1782.

TO THE REVEREND

THE HEADS OF COLLEGES,

THE FOLLOWING SERMONS,

PREACHED

AT THEIR APPOINTMENT,

ARE,

WITH GREAT RESPECT,

INSCRIBED.

Extract from the last Will and Testament of the late Reverend JOHN BAMPTON, *Canon of* Salisbury.

——— " I give and bequeath my Lands
" and Estates to the Chancellor, Masters,
" and Scholars of the University of Oxford
" for ever, to have and to hold all and sin-
" gular the said Lands or Estates upon trust,
" and to the intents and purposes herein after-
" mentioned; that is to say, I will and ap-
" point, that the Vice-Chancellor of the
" University of Oxford for the time being
" shall take and receive all the rents, issues,
" and profits thereof, and (after all taxes,
" reparations, and necessary deductions made)
" that he pay all the remainder to the en-
" dowment of eight Divinity Lecture Ser-
" mons, to be established for ever in the said
" University, and to be performed in the
" manner following:

" I direct and appoint, that, upon the first
" Tuesday in Easter Term, a Lecturer be
" yearly chosen by the Heads of Colleges
" only, and by no others, in the room ad-
" joining to the Printing-House, between

" the hours of ten in the morning and two
" in the afternoon, to preach eight Divinity
" Lecture Sermons, the year following, at
" St. Mary's in Oxford, between the com-
" mencement of the laſt month in Lent
" Term, and the end of the third week in
" Act Term.

" Alſo I direct and appoint, that the eight
" Divinity Lecture Sermons ſhall be preach-
" ed upon either of the following ſubjects
" — to confirm and eſtabliſh the Chriſtian
" Faith, and to confute all heretics and ſchiſ-
" matics—upon the divine authority of the
" Holy Scriptures — upon the authority of
" the writings of the primitive Fathers, as
" to the faith and practice of the primitive
" Church — upon the Divinity of our Lord
" and Saviour Jeſus Chriſt — upon the Divi-
" nity of the Holy Ghoſt — upon the Articles
" of the Chriſtian Faith, as comprehended
" in the Apoſtles' and Nicene Creeds.

" Alſo I direct, that thirty copies of the
" eight Divinity Lecture Sermons ſhall be
" always printed, within two months after
" they are preached, and one copy ſhall be
" given to the Chancellor of the Univerſity,
" and

"and one copy to the Head of every College, and one copy to the Mayor of the City of Oxford, and one copy to be put into the Bodleian Library; and the expence of printing them shall be paid out of the revenue of the Lands or Estates given for establishing the Divinity Lecture Sermons; and the Preacher shall not be paid, nor be entitled to the revenue, before they are printed.

"Also I direct and appoint, that no person shall be qualified to preach the Divinity Lecture Sermons, unless he hath taken the Degree of Master of Arts at least, in one of the two Universities of Oxford or Cambridge; and that the same person shall never preach the Divinity Lecture Sermons twice."

PRINCIPAL CONTENTS.

SERMON I.

Luke iii. 3, 4.

The word of the Lord came unto John, the Son of Zacharias, in the wilderness; and he came into all the country about Jordan, preaching the Baptism of Repentance.

General design, pag. 6.——Substance of the first discourse, ibid.—— I. The Jews admitted that John was a prophet, 7.—— the account, given of him by Josephus, correspondent to that by the Evangelists, 8. —— John called a prophet by Josippon, 9.——believed to be a prophet, without any view to the Messiah, ib.— this shewn from the Gospels, and Acts of the Apostles, ibid.——II. upon what evidence the prophetical character of John could be acknowledged, without connecting him with the Messiah, 10.—— 1. the outward appearances of a prophetical character in John, ibid. —— 2. his ministry of Baptism, and his call to Repentance, ibid. —— 3. the universal expectation of the Messiah, 13.—— 4. miraculous circumstances attending the conception and infancy of John, ib. —— from all these circumstances, arose a just presumption, but not a certainty, that John was a prophet, 15.—III. the true criterion of his inspiration, 16.——it was prophecy, with nearly present accomplishment, 19. —— illustration of this point, 20. —— the connection, between the Baptist and the Messiah, necessary, 21. —— John, not a prophet, unless he was the Messiah's forerunner, last page.

SER-

CONTENTS.

SERMON II.

Matth. iii. 5, 6.

Then went out to him Jerusalem, and all Judæa, and all the region round about Jordan, and were baptized of him in Jordan, confessing their sins.

John, sent to prepare the way of the Lord, pag. 24. —— to be shewn partly in this discourse, from the baptismal doctrine, as it respected the kingdom of heaven, and the Jewish people, ibid. —— import of the notice, the kingdom of heaven is at hand, 25. —— Jewish notions of that kingdom, ib. the true notion of it implied in John's preaching the baptism of repentance, 27. —— a caution attributed to the Baptist by Josephus, with respect to his baptism, 29. —— the ministry of the Baptist proceeded upon principles, exclusive of the Law, and entirely Evangelical, 32. —— hence he appears an original prophet, 33. —— particular view of the clauses in the baptismal doctrine of John, 34. —— he predicted the destruction of Israel, 36. —— the original circumstances, in this prophecy, shewed him a real prophet, 37. —— he predicted the rejection of Israel, and the call of the Gentiles, 38. —— hence also he appeared an original prophet, 41. —— his baptismal doctrine levelled against the Jewish corruptions of the Scripture-sense, 43. —— he taught that the Messiah's kingdom, the true righteousness, the promise, and the genuine sonship to Abraham, were all spiritual, 44. —— inference, that he was a real prophet, to the end.

SERMON III.

Mark i. 7.

There cometh One, Mightier than I, after me.

Further

CONTENTS.

Further view of the baptismal doctrine, viz. as it related directly to the Messiah, pag. 48. —— the baptismal doctrine, as it stands in the text of Saint Matthew, resumed, 49. —— the attribute of power, ascribed to the Messiah, by the Baptist, 50. —— that of baptizing with the Holy Ghost, ibid. —— that of transcendent dignity, 51. —— John ascribed these attributes to the Messiah, by divine revelation vouchsafed to himself, 52. —— evidences of this, from his additions to the prophecies relating to the person of the Messiah, 53. —— the Baptist represents the Messiah as the judge of all the world, 58. —— summary view of the baptismal doctrine, 63. —— shewn to have been delivered, while the Messiah remained unknown to the Baptist, 64. —— the words, " I knew him not," considered, 66, to the end.

SERMON IV.

John i. 6, 7.

There was a man, sent from God, whose name was John — the same came for a witness —

Of the testimonies of John, after he knew, who was the Messiah, 74. —— of the baptism of Jesus by him, ibid. —— upon this John ceased to be simply the forerunner, and became a witness, 75. —— the assertion, " I knew him not," may be extended, as far as this interview, but not beyond it, ibid. —— the Messiah notified to the Baptist by immediate revelation, 76. —— instances similar to this, ibid. —— proofs in the conduct of John, at Jordan, that he knew Jesus was the Messiah, 77. —some particulars, not revealed to the Baptist, before this interview, 79. —— observations, on this transaction, pursued, 80. —— the descent of the Spirit upon Jesus, 81. —— the Voice of the Father from heaven, 82. —— The first testimony of John, after his baptizing Jesus, This was he, &c. and observations upon it, 84.——the attribute of preexistence now first assigned, 85. —— appears grounded on the direct interpretation of the title, Son of God, ibid. —— Deputation of priests and Levites to John, and the extent and import of his answer to their enquiries, 87. —— Jesus, returned from the temptation, presents himself again to John, 89, —— ob-
servations

servations on the character, Lamb of God, then applied to him by the Baptist, ibid. —— illustration of John i. 30, and the subsequent verses, 92, —— inferences from the preceding observations, pag. 98.

SERMON V.

John i. 7.

The same came for a witness, to bear witness of the light, that all men through him might believe.

Illustrations of the doctrine of John, as a witness, continued, 99. —— on the character, Son of God, 100. —— in what sense John applied it to Jesus, 101. —— the capital testimony of the Baptist, John iii. 26, &c. considered, ib. —— the whole character of the Messiah displayed by the Baptist in this testimony, in more magnificent terms, than he had employed before, 107. —— they were consonant to the sense of ancient Scripture, but unknown in Israel, 108. —— some of these characters imply in what sense he applied the title, Son of God, ibid. —— summary view of the whole ministry of John hitherto, 109. —— considered as a witness, in his imprisonment, 111. —— his sending the disciples to Jesus illustrated, 112. —— concluding inference that John was Elias, 121.

SERMON VI.

John xiii. 19.

Now I tell you, before it come, that when it is come to pass, ye may believe that I am He.

The completion of the prophecy of John, as Forerunner, and of his testimony, as a Witness, to be shewn, from prophecies

of

CONTENTS.

of Jesus, either relating to characters ascribed to him by John, or parallel to prophecies of the Baptist, 124. ——— prophecies, to be considered in this discourse, relate to characters, which John had assigned, ibid. ——— 1st Character, the attribute of power to the Messiah, " he that cometh after me is mightier than I." 125. ——— reflections on the reality of the miracles of Jesus, ibid.———view of his miracles, as admitting a prophetical application, or giving him immediate occasion to deliver prophecies, 129.———inferences from the foregoing observations, 134.———II. The character, Lamb of God, and the prophecies of Jesus, relating to it, ib. ——— predicts his passion, and its circumstances, 135. ——— most of these prophecies original, 136. ——— inferences from the foregoing observations, 142.———III. The character Son of God, and the prophecy of his resurrection, that related to it, 144. ——— original circumstances in that prophecy, 145.———from these, Jesus appeared a prophet, 146. ——— his promise to rise again by his own power shews him more than a prophet, ibid. ——— illustration of that promise, 147. ——— inference from foregoing observations, 149.—IV. The prophecy which Jesus gave of his own ascension, justifies the testimony of John, that he came from above, 150. ——— original circumstance, in that prophecy, ibid. ——— general inference from the substance of this discourse, 152.

SERMON VII.

John xiii. 19.

Now I tell you, before it come, that when it is come to pass, ye may believe that I am He.

Of the prophecies of Jesus, that were parallel to those of John, ——— I. Christ spoke of the restoration of the Holy Spirit, in the terms both of a prophecy and a promise, 154. ——— he represented the Holy Spirit, as another divine agent in the work of redemption, 155. ——— inferences from the parting address of Jesus to the disciples, ibid. ——— of the terms, in which Jesus repeated the same prophecy, after his resurrection, 157. ——— parallel to the prophecy delivered by John,

John, " he shall baptize you." &c. ibid. —— and to the language of the ancient prophets, yet original in Jesus, 158.—— inferences from the foregoing remarks on this prophecy, 159. ——II. The prophecy of Jesus, of the conversion of the Gentiles, parallel to the prophetical admonition of John, " think not to say within yourselves. &c." 161. —— this prophecy original in Jesus, 163. —— shewn first, from comparing his conduct, as a teacher of Israel, with his prediction that the Gentiles should be converted, 164.——2dly, from his words, " Thou art Peter, and upon this rock, I will build my church;" " and, I will give unto thee the keys of the kingdom of heaven," 172.——III. The prophecy of Jesus, of the destruction of Israel, parallel to the prophecy of John, " now the axe is laid unto the root of the trees," 176. —— and to those of ancient prophets, ibid. —— yet shewn original in Christ, from some new circumstances, which he interwove with the prediction, 177. —— 1. the completion of it limited to a particular generation, and period of time, ibid. —— 2. prophetical history of the period between the delivery and the accomplishment of the prophecy, 178. —— 3. That his elect should be then the objects of divine protection, 179. —— 4. the captivity of the Jews in all nations, and the present state of Jerusalem, predicted, and the captivity of the one, and the desolation of the other, limited to a particular period, 180.—— Jewish imprecation, " his blood be on us, and on our children," thus literally fulfilled, 181. —— this first act of our Lord's judgement upon Israel, prefigures his last universal one over the world, 182. —— both called in Scripture his coming, ibid.——Jesus, in the same prophecy. (Matth. xxiv.) and the Baptist, in the clause, " whose fan is in his hand, &c," speak primarily of the judgement of Israel, and ultimately of the judgement of the world, 183. —— other prophecies by Jesus of his universal judgement, 184. —— inferences from the substance of this discourse, ibid.

SERMON VIII.

John xiii. 19.

Now I tell you, before it come, that when it is come to pass, ye may believe that I am he.

CONTENTS.

Of the prophecy, which Jesus delivered, of the prevalence of his Gospel, 187.—— the old prophets, the Baptist, and Jesus himself, prophetically characterized the unpromising rise, but final fulness of the Messiah's kingdom, 188.—— the prevalence of the Gospel, proves Christ a prophet; but as it must be ascribed only to his own accomplishment of his promises, it proves him, more than a prophet, 189, &c.—— I. The Apostles, on Christ's leaving them, had not sufficient knowledge for their office, 191.—— nor sufficient fortitude, ibid. sq.——Jesus foretold their sufferings and violent death, 191.—— reflection on this prophecy, 193.——notwithstanding their deficiencies, the Apostles actually entered on their ministry, within a few days after their Lord's departure, 194. —— hence necessarily concluded, that their deficiencies were previously remedied, 195. —— not by their own natural powers, ibid.—— but by the coming of the Holy Ghost upon them, 196. —— He brought the Gospel down from heaven, 199. —— the Apostles stood in need of further illumination afterwards, ibid. —— II. The continuance of the Law, another obstacle, 200.——effects of it on the minds of the Jews, ibid. —— promise of Jesus to remove this obstacle, 202.—— fulfilled in the fall of Jerusalem and the temple, and in the dispersion of the Jews, 203. —— Jesus marked this accomplishment of his denunciation of woe to Israel, as immediately leading to the general establishment of his Gospel, 206.—under Hadrian, the Jews endeavoured, in vain, to recover their holy place, ibid. —— Julian endeavoured, in vain, to rebuild it, 207. —— III. Satan's kingdom another obstacle to the establishment of the kingdom of Jesus, 208. —— he gave his disciples power, and promised them support from himself, against this enemy, 209.—— inferences from the substance of this discourse, 210.—— General conclusions from all the discourses, 202. —— prophecies of Jesus ascribable only to the divine Spirit; and the exact accomplishment of them, as they stand in the Gospels, ascribable only to the divine power, 216. —— conclusion, that God set his seal upon the Gospel, both as it was preached by Jesus, and as it was published in writing by the Evangelists.

SERMON I.

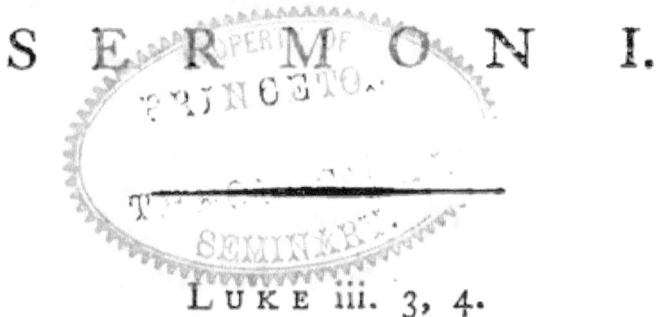

LUKE iii. 3, 4.

The word of the Lord came unto John, the Son of Zacharias, in the wilderness; and he came into all the country about Jordan, preaching the Baptism of Repentance.

THE history of Christ was admirably adapted to give, the most clear and venerable representation of Christianity, and, at the same time, an obvious and frequent [a] demonstration of its truth. For, as the system of duty, contained in his moral and religious discourses, was in him visibly exemplified; so also, a considerable part of the evidence, that he came from God, arises from the several acts and incidents of his publick life. There are two questions, that

---

[a] An answer is given to the inquiry, why Christianity was delivered, in the history of our Saviour, in preference to any other form, in a Commencement Sermon, Jeffery's Tracts. Vol. ii. at the end.

have immediate reference to them; the one, concerning their real existence, and the other, respecting the proofs, which they afford of a divine attestation.

It may be observed, as to the reality of those facts, in the life of Christ, upon which his Religion is founded, that the testimony of friends and adversaries, has enabled us to trace the profession of Christianity, through all the intermediate ages, from our own times [b] till it began. During that long interval, it will be found invariably distinguished, with the observance of the same stated day of worship, and with the use of particular Sacraments, either in express memorial of different acts in the life of Christ, or in pursuance of his positive institution.

This [c] uninterrupted continuance of the Christian profession, accompanied with these characteristical observances, in all conjunctures of things, and against all obstacles, through the several ages, between the present time and that of Tiberius, evidently implies, that, in

---

[b] The prevalence of it, in Trajan's time, is attested by Plin. Ep. 97. Lib. 10. See also Daubuz pro testimonio Josephi. —Tacit. Annal. Lib. 15. cap. 44.—Sueton. Claud. cap. 25.—Julian. apud Cyrill. Lib. 6.

[c] This argument is drawn out at large by Dr. Campbell in his Authenticity of the Gospel History.

SERMON I.

his days, such persons first appeared as the disciples of Christ, and publickly asserted, that they heard the doctrines, and beheld the facts, upon which he founded, and 'commissioned them to advance, the Christian Religion.

By ᵈtheir hands, or under the immediate direction and revisal of some in their number, written histories were drawn up, and were received and used by the rest, as true narratives of what they had all heard and seen, during their intercourse with Christ.—So far as to the real existence of the facts, upon which Christianity depends.

That the Gospels, extant at this day, are the genuine histories, which these witnesses, immediately conversant with Jesus, either penned or approved, may be grounded, not only upon the testimony of heathen adversaries, and Christian apologists, in every age, but also, as a celebrated ᵉ writer observes, "upon the general reception and credit, which they found, not only in all the churches, but with all the private Christians of those ages, who were able to purchase copies of them; among whom,

---

ᶜ This is admitted by Julian, apud Cyrill. Lib. 9. 291.
ᵈ See Le Clerc's 3d. Dissert. subjoined to his Evang. Harm.
ᵉ Middleton. Free Inquiry, 4to. Ed. p. 155.

though it might perhaps be the defire of a few to corrupt, yet it was the common intereft of all, to preferve, and of none, to deftroy them. And we find accordingly, that they were guarded by all with the ftricteft care, fo as to be concealed from the knowledge and fearch of their heathen adverfaries, who alone were defirous to extirpate them. After fuch a publication therefore, and wide difperfion of them from their very origin, it is hardly poffible, that they fhould either be corrupted, or fuppreffed, or counterfeited, by a few, of what character or abilities foever; or that, according to the natural courfe of things, they fhould not be handed down from age to age, in the fame manner, with the works of all the other ancient writers of Greece and Rome; which, though tranfmitted through the hands of many profligate and faithlefs generations of men, yet have fuffered no diminution of their credit on that account; for though in every age there were feveral perhaps, who, from crafty and felfifh motives, might be difpofed to deprave, or even to fupprefs, fome particular books, yet their malice could reach only to a few copies, and would be reftrained therefore from the attempt, or

corrected

SERMON I.

corrected at least after the attempt, by the greater number of the same books, which were out of their reach, and remained still incorrupt. But besides all this, there were some circumstances, peculiar to the books of the New Testament, which ensured the preservation of them more effectually, than of any other ancient books whatsoever; the divinity of their character, and the religious regard, which was paid to them by all the sects and parties of Christians; and above all, the mutual jealousies of those very parties, which were perpetually watching over each other, lest any of them should corrupt the sources of that pure doctrine, which they all professed to teach and to deduce from the same books—it was not in the power of any craft, to impose spurious pieces, in the room of those genuine ones, which were actually deposited in all churches, and preserved, with the utmost reverence, in the hands of so many private Christians."

After these preliminary observations, to justify, in some measure, the liberty, that will be taken, of appealing to the Evangelical writings, as authentick histories of real fact, I proceed, in discharge of the honourable province assigned me, to shew that they contain

tain evidences of a divine atteſtation to the Goſpel, and begin with ſtating the drift and ſubſtance of the argument, to be purſued in theſe diſcourſes.

The deſign is; to produce and illuſtrate, firſt, the prophetical teſtimony of John the Baptiſt to the Goſpel, and its Author; and then, the principal prophecies of Chriſt himſelf; and to urge them jointly in ſupport of the divine original of the Chriſtian Religion.

This is the general ſcheme in view; the particular argument of each diſcourſe will be ſtated, as it occurs;—the ſequel of this will be employed to ſhew, firſt, that the Jews really admitted the prophetical character of the Baptiſt; ſecondly, that the evidence, upon which they admitted it, was only partial and preſumptive, the complete and deciſive proof of it being entirely diſregarded; and laſtly, to point out from whence the true and concluſive evidence of his divine miſſion aroſe.

I. With reſpect to the general reception of John as a prophet, it may be obſerved, that ᶠ Jewiſh hiſtorians atteſt his adminiſtration of baptiſm, and appropriate to him that title, drawn from his office, by which he is diſ-

---

ᶠ Joſephus, and Joſeph ben Gorion, or Joſippon. See Lardner, Jewiſh and Heathen Teſtimonies.

tinguiſhed

tinguished in the Gospels, and assign the reign of Herod Antipas, as the date, and the land of Judæa, as the scene, of his ministry, and further intimate that a multitude of Jews received his baptism.

The testimony, given by Josephus in particular, to the publick ministry and general veneration of the Baptist, will have the greater weight in behalf of the Gospel, which began in the baptism of John, from the agreement, subsisting between the sacred writers and him, in their account, not only of the ministry and extraordinary success of the Baptist, but also of other circumstances, respecting the character and the objects of his baptism, of which notice will be taken hereafter.

This historian informs us, that John had conciliated the affection and reverence of the people to so great a degree, that his popularity alarmed the king; and that the destruction of his army was publickly reputed a just act of divine vengeance against him, for shedding the blood of John.

Agreeably to this account, we learn from the Gospels, that Herod, although he ventured to shut up John in prison, yet permitted his disciples to continue their intercourse with him, and for a long time, through ᶠ fear of the

ᶠ Matth. xiv. 5.

the people and ᶠperſonal reſpect to the Baptiſt, forbore to deprive him of life, and, at laſt, gave him up with the greateſt reluctance to the ſanguinary malice of Herodias.

The great Council of the Jews, who aſſumed and exerciſed the right of examining and determining every claim to a prophetical commiſſion, by a ſolemn deputation of Levites to the Baptiſt, enquired into the truth of his pretenſions. The turn of their queſtions implies a perſuaſion in the meſſengers, that John was a real prophet; art thou Elias, or that prophet, or the Chriſt? They did not enquire, whether God had ſent him, but rather, in what divine character he came; and they did not demand, " why baptizeſt thou then," untill he had already diſclaimed, one after another, the ſeveral divine characters, which they had imagined might belong to him. And after all, though his anſwer gave offence to the Council, yet they did not venture to condemn him as a falſe prophet. Indeed, the danger was great of diſowning his miſſion from God, and depreciating his baptiſm; " ᵍif we ſhall ſay, it was of men, all the people will ſtone us, for they be perſuaded that John was a prophet," is the language held by themſelves.

ᶠ Mark vi. 20.   ᵍ Luke xx. 5, 6.

The principal circumstances, which can be drawn, either from the Scripture, or the account of Josephus, have sufficient agreement, to shew, that the character of the Baptist was generally believed prophetical. The ᶠ latest of the two Jewish historians expressly calls him a prophet; and, whether this writer was a Jew in reality, or in pretence only, it seems to be equally certain, that he has given the true Jewish opinion concerning John. If he is esteemed a real Jew, then he ought also to be reckoned a credible judge and witness of the current notions of his countrymen; but, on the contrary, if it be supposed, that he personated a Jewish character, and that in a very late period, it may then be observed, that the reception and credit of his history among the Jews, even in preference to that of Josephus, sufficiently shews, that they justify and authenticate the substance of his story.

This belief, of the inspiration of John, seems to have been generally entertained without any view to the Messiah. For, ᵍ in the Gospels, mention is made of disciples, that still adhered to, and visited, the Baptist in the prison, when Christ was in the full exercise

---

ᶠ Josippon is supposed to have written about the eleventh century. Lardner, ubi supra —— ᵍ Matth. ix. 14. xi. 2.

of his ministry; and of others, who observed exactly the frequent fasts, that John had prescribed, and, as it appears, blamed Christ and his followers, for their disuse of similar restrictions. We find also, ^e in the Acts of the Apostles, that Apollos, and some Jews, whom St. Paul met with at Ephesus, knew, and had received, only the baptism of John.

All the Jews of this description, as they seem to have believed the prophetical character of the Baptist, could have no other ground for admitting it, except that, upon which he was separately considered, and independent of the Messiah. The immediate question then will be, upon what evidence the inspiration of John was acknowledged by those, who either overlooked, or violated, the connection between him and Christ; and, whether that evidence was, or was not, sufficient to justify, in the fullest extent, the conclusion they drew. And, as this was the second of the three articles, proposed for present consideration, I endeavour, in the next place, if it be possible, to assign some of their reasons.

II. 1. In the plainness of his habit, and the exact abstinence of his life, which are distinctly ^f marked by the Evangelists, the Baptist

^e xviii. 24. xix. 2.   ^f See Grotius on Matth. iii. 4. Compare Zech. xiii. 4. 2 Kings i. 8. 1 Chron. xxi. 16.   carried

carried all the outward appearances of a prophetical character. His diftinguifhed holinefs, and the fervent and authoritative ftyle, in which he rebuked the vices and the finners of his time, would naturally engage the utmoft refpect and veneration of all, that were religioufly difpofed. And, as the communication between God and his people, feemed to be renewed of late, by the return of a miraculous power at the waters of [f] Bethefda, they would perhaps be the more readily inclined, to expect the revival of prophecy among them, and, on finding the [g] reputed characteriftics of a prophetical fpirit in the Baptift, to attribute infpiration to him.

2. This impreffion, in favour of John, might alfo be confirmed, by his miniftry of Baptifm, and his call to Repentance. For their own principles would naturally difpofe them to take efpeciall notice of both thefe particulars.

Baptifm was a facrament of the Jews, and was adminiftered by John in the cuftomary

---

[f] John v. 4.
[g] Vorftius enumerates fix concomitants or antecedents of prophecy——among them were; Sequeftration from the common and profane manner of living——Seafonablenefs of the time: for they held all times not equally feafonable. ad Maimonid. de fund. Leg. c. 7.

form.

form. Their fathers had been baptized unto
[h] Moses, or unto that dispensation of religion
and worship, which God established among
them by his ministry; and as, under the Law
of Moses, the " old world," as they termed
it, Baptism had been their sacrament of original admission; so also, from their construction of the prophecies, and from popular
tradition, they looked for the same means of
[i] initiation to the "[k] new world" under the
Messiah.   The call to Repentance agreed
equally with their preconceptions. The
maxim was received among them[l], If Israel
repent but one day, presently the Redeemer
cometh. Whether they entertained just notions of Baptism and Repentance, or otherwise, is not considered here; but the present
question is, simply, whether the use of Baptism, and the call to Repentance, were likely
to be deemed the accomplishment of their
own traditions, and, on that account, apparent indications of a prophetical spirit in the

---

[h] 1 Corinth. x. 2.—— Heb. ix. 19.—— Lightfoot Har.
1 Part, pag. 466.
[i] See Grot. on John i. 25. — But a baptism, like that of
John, to initiate them to a new Religion, seems not to have
been expected.
[k] Lightfoot. Har. 1st part, pag. 9. et passim.
[l] Lightfoot, Vol. 2. Har. 1st part, pag. 10.

Baptist;

Baptist; and this perhaps may be conceiveable.

3. But the presumption of the inspiration of John, in whatsoever degree the circumstances, hitherto mentioned, can be supposed to have suggested it, would be considerably strengthened by the universal expectation of the Messiah. Syria had been subdued, and annexed to the great empire of Rome; and, as the time, limited in the prophecy of [m] Daniel, was confessedly elapsed, the Kingdom of the God of heaven, which he had foretold, under Messiah the Prince, was immediately expected to appear. The universal prevalence of this expectation in Israel, at that time, has been indisputably shewn by writers both [n] sacred and profane. "The kingdom of heaven is at hand," was therefore a notice, likely to further every previous supposition of an inspired character in the Baptist.

4. But above all, the miraculous circumstances, that attended the conception, and infancy, of John, if generally known, would greatly facilitate his admission, as a prophet.

---

[m] Chap. 9.
[n] Luke xix. 11. Sueton. in Vesp. c. 4.

When they originally happened, "° fear came on all, and these sayings were noised abroad throughout all the hill-country, and all they that had heard them, laid them up in their hearts, saying, what manner of child shall this be?" The report of these circumstances might be revived, upon the coming of John to baptize, so near those parts; and, as the people grew daily more and more disposed to muse and enquire concerning him, a knowledge of them would be likely to take a wider extent. If so, as it would immediately occur, that John [p] was of the line of Aaron, and by right of birth a priest of the God of Israel, as [q] Josippon expressly calls him, these miraculous circumstances would indeed have a powerfull effect, in persuading the publick, that his baptism was from heaven, and not of men.—Indeed, neither of the prophecies, by the [r] Angel and [s] Zacharias, respecting the real office of John, seem to have been regarded or known. If that had been the case, his true character, and the relation between him and the Messias, could scarcely have passed, as it did, without notice

---

° Luke i. 65.   [p] Luke i. 1.
[q] Gorionides Joannem hunc prophetam vocat. Grot. ad Matth. xi. 9.   [r] Luke i. 17.   [s] Luke i. 76.

and

and effect. But still, even a rumour, however indistinct, that the birth of the Baptist had been foretold, and his name dictated, by an Angel, that appeared to Zacharias, during his sacerdotal course in the Temple, would add very confiderable weight to every other fuppofed evidence of his infpiration, and might poffibly determine the Jews, without further hefitation, to admit his prophetical character.

If then, the real ftate of the Jewifh opinions and expectations, at the time, be confidered, thefe feveral circumftances, taken in aid of each other, will probably appear fufficient to have raifed a general prefumption, that John was a prophet[t]; and, that they fhould operate fo far, as to attach the people to him, and difpofe them to receive his baptifm, in the true fpirit of it, and to expect, with repentance and faith, the coming of the Meffias, whom he predicted, feems to have been the divine intention.

But then, to treat this prefumption, as if it was abfolute certainty, and to admit the prophetical character of the Baptift, upon this probable evidence, exclufive of all other, to

[t] His fuccefs, even in that partial degree, to which it extended, was the completion of prophecy. Malachi. 4. 5, 6. Luke i. 17.

be given in future, tended immediately to contradict the counsel of God. It led many of the Jews to break the necessary connection between the Baptist and the Messias, and to look no farther than John; and of course, they must have acquiesced in such evidence of his inspiration, as their limited view afforded. But all their proofs of the prophetical character of John, supposing him singly considered, whether they arose from the circumstances, already recited, or from any other, fell short of that complete and decisive evidence, which God had provided; and when they admitted John, as a prophet, upon any presumptive ground alone, however strong, they had much yet to learn, both of his credentials and his office. His inspiration could be absolutely ascertained, only by another, and a subsequent, criterion; and what that was, is a material question, and will make the third and final article of the present enquiry.

III. The usual means of authenticating a divine mission, were not given to John. He did no miracle; and, on that account, if he really was the messenger of God, we may expect other evidence, upon which his prophetical character could be, and therefore ought

to

SERMON I.

to have been, determined. If he had no such decisive evidence in his favour, however strong a presumption, of his divine commission, might arise from other circumstances, yet must it lie open to question, as God never failed to give an indisputable attestation to every real prophet. Upon that footing, the Baptist, as not being invested with a miraculous power, would have been left without any conclusive evidence of his mission from God; and the Jews, if their own experience, in the cases of former prophets, had influenced their judgement, would, have questioned the prophetical character of any claimant, who wanted the means of proving it undeniably certain, and could only render it probable.

The truth, in the case before us, appears to be this. The providence of God, as if to prevent the very mistake, which was made by the Jews, did not authenticate the mission of John, by any indubitable proof, that was exclusively personal to the Baptist, as the power of working miracles would have been. The only decisive evidence, that John was a real prophet, arose out of his relation to the Messias; in him it began, and was reflected back upon the Baptist. It was his appointed province to prepare the way for One Mightier, that should come, and to make him manifest unto Israel. The unquestionable right of the Baptist to a prophetical character, could therefore be shewn, only by the absolute appearance of that Mightier One, for whom he prepared the way. If he had spoken of One to come, who came not; or had appropriated characters to him, which, if he came, he did not sustain; or had attributed works to him, which he did not accomplish, it would have been reasonably concluded, in opposition to all other evidence, that he really bore no divine commission. But, on the contrary, if the predictions of the Baptist, concerning the speedy appearance, office, and works of Him, who was to come, were verified; in that accomplishment would consist the proper and sufficient proof, that John himself was a prophet; and his testimony to the Messias, upon his appearance, ought then to have disposed the people of those and of all succeeding times, to believe the divine commission of both.

According to this representation, though the usual evidence of miracles, was not the appointed proof, that the word of the Lord came to John, yet another, and that decisive in the question, was granted to him. This was

was prophecy; but not of such a cast, as to leave the point, which it was intended to ascertain, for a considerable interval of time, in suspence and undetermined. It was prophecy, not with remote, but nearly present, accomplishment; it was not as a light, shining long in a dark place, but the dawn hasted on, and the day-star soon arose. The matter was placed upon the proper ground, by some of the Jews, in one instance, which is thus recorded by the Evangelist. " ^u Jesus went away again beyond Jordan, unto the place, where John at first baptized, and there he abode. And many resorted unto him, and said, John did no miracle; but all things, that John spake of this man, were true." The place reminded them of former testimonies to the Messias, which they had heard the Baptist deliver there; and this recollection produced in them a natural and reasonable effect, for the Evangelist adds, " and many believed on him there." They saw and felt the true evidence of the prophetical character of John, and were immediately led, by their just views, to proceed one step further than many

---

^u John x. 41, 42.—See Chemnit. H. E. B. 5. pag. 10.

of their countrymen, and to admit the divine miſſion of Chriſt, as well as that of John.

I have thus endeavoured to ſhew, that the ground, upon which thoſe Jews, who looked no farther than the Baptiſt, attributed an inſpired character to him, was partial; and have ſtated what appears the full evidence of it, to which they ought to have extended their views; that it might be diſtinctly ſeen, with what admirable ſtrictneſs, the credentials of the Baptiſt were adjuſted to the nature and deſign of his office. And, as this point ſeems of conſequence in any account of the teſtimony of the Baptiſt to Jeſus, this diſcourſe ſhall be cloſed with a ſhort illuſtration of it.

Many prophets, and eſpecially Elias, in whoſe ſpirit and power the Baptiſt came, had been permitted to work miracles. They ſtood as ſingle objects; and the public attention was to be drawn, and continued, to them alone. The exerciſe of a miraculous power would therefore directly facilitate their admiſſion, in the character of divine meſſengers. But the caſe was otherwiſe with the Baptiſt. The exerciſe of a miraculous power, as it muſt tend to fix the eyes of the people immoveably upon him, would have counteracted the real purpoſe of his office, which was intended

tended to manifest another unto Israel. And, as the Jews stood most in need of an inducement to look beyond the Baptist, the conclusive evidence of his divine mission, was of that particular nature, which was best calculated to carry their views forward to the Messias.

A persuasion that John really was a prophet, generally prevailed; this seems to be clear from the Jewish historians. But the Scriptures alone assign the ground, upon which that persuasion could be completely justified. According to them, neither the prophetical notice, given by the Baptist, "the kingdom of heaven is at hand," nor the preceding prophecies of the Angel and Zacharias, could be verified, except in the actual coming of the Messiah; and all decisive evidence, of the inspiration of John, would therefore, as it seems, be excluded, if the Baptist was considered independent of him.

A necessary connection appears then to have subsisted between them; and their credentials seem to have been unavoidably involved so far, that the divine mission of both was to be ascertained, at one instant, and in one event. The Baptist came in the character of forerunner; and it was not possible to prove him, even a prophet, except from that very incident, which would alſo prove him the Forerunner. So evidently was it provided, that the Baptiſt could not fail to authenticate the divine miſſion of the Meſſias, by the ſame means, and in the ſame degree, wherein he eſtabliſhed his own.

The credibility of the Goſpel-hiſtory of the Baptiſt will perhaps be confirmed, and his teſtimony to Jeſus enforced, if it has now been ſhewn with any ſucceſs, that, although John certainly was received as a prophet, yet his character could not be proved prophetical, if it were any other, except that, which the Goſpel-writers repreſent it, of Forerunner to the Meſſiah.

SERMON II.

MATT. iii. 5, 6.

Then went out to him Jerusalem, and all Judæa, and all the region round about Jordan, and were baptized of him in Jordan, confessing their sins.

THE divine mission of the Baptist, however strongly it might be presumed, could not, as I have before endeavoured to shew, be completely ascertained, if he were considered singly, and independent of the Messias. If he did not really bear that character of Forerunner to One Mightier, who was to come, which the Gospel-writers attribute to him, no decisive evidence seems assignable, that he came from God.

This point having been discussed in the preceding discourse, I proceed to shew, that sufficient evidences of his [a] prophetical character might have been discovered, and accumulated, by considering him as a messenger, sent to prepare the way of the Lord.

This will be attempted only in part, at present, by illustrating the baptismal doctrine of John, as far as it respected the kingdom of heaven, and the people of Israel.

I. As John, by both his parents, was of the line of Aaron, he was by right of birth a priest of the God of Israel. When he attained the proper age for commencing his ministry, he declined the service of the Sanctuary, and forsook the Church of Israel; but assumed, and publickly exercised, a sacerdotal office, in obedience, as he professed, to the word of the Lord. Baptism was the only one of the Jewish ceremonies, which he

---

[a] Evidence of a divine mission may arise from one or more of the following circumstances. 1st, From explaining former prophecies, so as to imply such a clear and comprehensive knowledge of the events, predicted therein, that it could not reasonably be ascribed to the unassisted faculties of man; Or, 2dly, from declaring that the accomplishment of prophecies was immediately approaching; Or, 3dly, from repeating the prophecies themselves, with new and additional circumstances; Or, lastly, from delivering predictions entirely original. Frequent occasion will arise of applying one or other of these criteria.——

retained

retained, but of this he kept only the form. The new and original purpose, to which he applied it, may be collected from his baptismal doctrine. The leading points of it shew, that the Holy Ghost, with which John had been filled from the womb, imparted to him just views of the religious state of Israel, at that time; and enabled him to predict the characteristical principles and nature of the Gospel-kingdom, which he declared to be at hand, together with the rejection of the Jews, and the admission of the Gentiles.

" The kingdom of heaven is at hand," was the awakening notice, upon which his baptismal exhortation was grounded. The expression itself was not strange to his hearers, nor the intelligence, which he gave them, unexpected. It coincided with the popular opinion, and as, in the Jewish sense, it was extremely pleasing, the completion of it was impatiently desired. We may therefore imagine, that the Baptist was readily understood to announce [b] the approach of the Mes-

---

[b] Matth. xii. 28. xvi. 19. Luke xvii. 20, 21. Lightfoot, Vol. 1. pag. 568. sq.—Whitby, Matth. iii. 2.— βασιλείαν ιϛκῦθαι τὴν παρουσίαν αὐτῦ (Χριϛῦ) τὴν τε πρωτέραν ἢ τὸν ἐχάτην λίγει. Chrysost. Hom. X. in Matth. loc. cit.

sias.

fias. The phrase seems to be thus interpreted in many passages of Scripture; and John applied it, in the greatest latitude, to denote the whole oeconomy of things under the Messias.

Indeed, the Baptist and his audience entirely disagreed in their notion of that state. The opinion, entertained of it by the Jews, may perhaps, on the authority of their own writers, as well as of the Scripture, be justly stated in the subsequent particulars.

They expected, that the [c] splendor and solemnity of their civil and religious constitution would then be raised to the [d] utmost height; and Scripture had been strained to justify that fond belief, which zeal for the law had suggested, and the voice of tradition confirmed. They presumed also, that the [e] dispersed of Israel would be gathered to-

---

[c] Maimonides says, the Jews expected, that the nations, roused at the exhortation of the Messias, would turn to the Law. See Lightfoot Harmony, 1st part. pag. 14.

[d] It was expected that the Messias should restore the kingdom of the house of David to its old glory, and build the temple, and bring home all the dispersed of Israel: and that Israel should then be at rest from the kingdom of wickedness, to study the Law and the Commandments without disquietude. Lightfoot, Vol. 1. p. 568, from Maimonides. Perhaps there are traces of this opinion in the Gospels. John xi. 52. ——

[e] John viii. 39. — It shall be the morning to Israel, but night to the nations of the world. —— Israel in the time to come

gether in their own land, and that the blessings of the Messiah's kingdom would be conferred upon them, by right of descent from Abraham, and in virtue of the divine promise, to the ᶠ exclusion of all other nations. They expected further, that the oppression of the kingdoms would then cease, and not only political liberty, but also political dominion, be restored to Israel.

Thus had they represented the kingdom of heaven to themselves; and that blindness of mind, and hardness of heart, for which they were reproved so severely, and have now suffered so long, may be ultimately resolved into these principles. How greatly they mistook their own religious state, and the nature of the Messiah's kingdom, the representation of both, given by the Baptist, will sufficiently discover.

He "preached, the Baptism of Repentance" —that, in use among the Jews, deserves rather to be named the baptism of strict obedience.

---

come (i. e. the days of the Messias) shall be left only, and there shall be with him no strange God,——are Jewish traditions, produced from their writers, by Lightfoot. Vol. 1. pag. 14.
ᶠ Luke xxiv. 21. Acts i. 6. —— Lardner. Cred. of G. H. B. 1. Ch. 5.

"This

"[g] This shall be thy thy righteousness," was the language of the law to the candidate for admission; and although the burden, to which he submitted, was grievous, yet the obligation incurred was strict. — " Cursed is every one, that continueth not in all things, which are written in the book of the law to do them." The ceremonial part of it at length engrossed the popular attention and reverence, and ritual obedience passed for true religion; and in direct conformity to this principle, it was imagined that Abraham obtained the promise through the righteousness of works. The notions of repentance, which they entertained, had not led them to admit any insufficiency in the legal atonements, or to feel and confess their sinful and unforgiven state. Among them it was, of course, merely formal, without power, and entirely unproductive of fruits, worthy of repentance.

Under this perversion of things, when the moral law had entirely declined in public esteem, repentance, in the true sense of it, could have no place, as a principle of action. Before it could operate, the current of the prevailing opinions must be turned, and a due

---

[g] Deuteron. iv. 1. vi. 25. xxvii. 26. xxx. 15. 19. Ezekiel. xx. 11. Galat. iii. 10. —

preference

SERMON II.

preference restored of the moral to the ritual law. This, among other effects, was reserved for a new dispensation, that would establish the righteousness of the heart, and not of the letter, and annex the divine sanction and blessing to a spiritual service.

The baptism of repentance, was strictly accommodated to a people in this state of moral corruption, and only to a dispensation of this cast; and when the Baptist accordingly proposed it, he not only acted from views, imparted to him by the Holy Spirit, of the depraved and unforgiven state of Israel, however weakly felt, or hardily disclaimed; but also, prophetically intimated, what was the great pervading principle and character of that dispensation, which he prepared them to receive; and represented it, not as a law of works, but as a kingdom of grace; for his baptism preceeded as a sign of repentance, and led on to subsequent remission of sin.

Josephus [k] attributes to the Baptist a caution, against a mistake that might be made, respecting the nature of his baptism, as it

---

[k] Joseph. Antiq. Iud. Lib. 18. cap. 7. Οὕτω γὰρ καὶ τὴν βάπτισιν ἀποδεκτὴν αὐτῷ (Θεῷ) φανεῖσθαι, μὴ ἐπί τινων ἁμαρτάδων παραιτήσει χρωμένων, ἀλλ᾽ ἐφ᾽ ἁγνείᾳ τοῦ σώματος, ἅτε δὴ καὶ τῆς ψυχῆς δικαιοσύνῃ προεκκεκαθαρμένης.

seems

seems, in this very particular. God would accept it, he taught, [1] in behalf of those "who did not use it, as an excuse for their sins, but as a means of bodily purification, implying a previous purification of the heart by righteousness." There is a remarkable similarity between the concluding part of this passage in Josephus, and the words of the Apostle [m] Peter, concerning baptism, "not the putting away of the filth of the flesh, but the answer of a good conscience toward God." And the representation of John's baptism, given by the Jewish writer, agrees with that of the Evangelists. They have not characterized it as the baptism of remission of sins, but simply of repentance, introductory to it. According to the prophecy of Zacharias, it was the office of the Baptist, "to give knowledge of salvation by the remission of sins;" but it is not said, that he was to give the salvation itself. He baptized with water unto repentance, [n] without presuming

---

[m] 1 Pet. iii. 21.

[n] Theophylact, on Matt. 3. "Ἄφεσιν ἁμαρτιῶν οὐκ εἶχε τὸ Ἰωάννου βάπτισμα, ἀλλὰ μόνην μετάνοιαν ἐκήρυττεν ὁ Ἰωάννης, καὶ εἰς ἄφεσιν ἁμαρτιῶν ἔφερεν, ἀντὶ τοῦ, εἰς τὸ τοῦ χριστοῦ βάπτισμα ὡδήγει, παρ' οὗ ἡ ἄφεσις τῶν ἁμαρτιῶν. See also Chrysostom Homil. 74. Tom. 5. pag. 535. Suicer. Thes. in voc. βάπτισμα.

to sanctify by the baptismal water, or to confer remission of sins upon repentance.

Josephus therefore sketches the real nature and spirit of John's baptism, as he supposes it to imply, by purification of the body, the previous purification of the heart. He states indeed only part of the truth; but he has preserved enough of it, to render his testimony valuable, and as far as it goes, it appears directly apposite. According to him, John cautioned the people, that his baptism had not any privilege of propitiating God for sin; and the Gospels inform us, that he ascribed this great prerogative to One Mightier, that should come. As it is agreed therefore, on both sides, that he disclaimed this privilege for himself, it seems fairly to result from the Jewish, as well as the Evangelical, history, that the baptism of John was simply of a preparatory nature, and that he really was only the forerunner of another.

But when he administered baptism, as introductory, in any degree, to the remission of sins, the question, whether the votaries of the law stood already in a state of salvation, was by him decided against the Jews. The legal purifications and atonements, which the original sanction of God, and the certainty,

they

they were prefumed to give, of acceptance and favour with him, had concurred to fupport and endear, were now depreciated, as invalid; and warning was given that juftification ° with God muft be fought for upon other terms. Every plea, grounded on obedience to the law, even fuppofing it had been exact, was evidently difallowed. John accordingly propofed, as an indifpenfable and univerfal requifite, the baptifm of repentance, to open the way to fubfequent remiffion of fins. It was a feal of the righteoufnefs of faith in the Meffias who was to come; and the acceptance and efficacy of it depended upon him, whofe blood would wafh away fin, and whofe baptifm of the fpirit would internally purify. As this was the main object of Faith, propofed by John to his difciples, of courfe, they who received his baptifm, ceafed to be under the law. It was the counfel of God to bring them into the path of falvation, and they who refolved to abide by their old principles and profeffion, would reject it againft themfelves.

Thus the miniftry of John proceeded upon principles exclufive of the law, and entirely

° βακραίτησιν ἁμαρτάδων, as Jofephus calls it.

Evangelical. Christ afterwards enforced them in his conference with Nicodemus; and the import of the Baptist's doctrine, appears extremely similar to the substance of that interesting conversation. That master of Israel knew not these things; a baptism of water, unto spiritual regeneration of heart, both in principles and practice, as preparatory to admission into the kingdom of the Messias, had never entered his mind; and, when proposed, it surpassed his apprehension. Indeed, none of the ancient prophecies, or of those which were nearest to this time, seem to have raised any expectation, that can be certainly traced, of such an extraordinary ministry, as that, undertaken by the Baptist; at least, a baptism, of this effect and import, was not known to be in the divine intention, till the calling of John. For the prophecies that characterized his office, as forerunner of the Lord, had not been so far particular, as to ascribe the use of baptism to him. The administration of it appears evidently to have been dictated to him by divine revelation, since the word of the Lord could alone enable him, prophetically to represent the kingdom of heaven, in direct contradiction to the Jewish construction of the prophecies, as a dispensation of spiritual grace and redemption, intended to supersede the ritual oeconomy of Moses.

The call to repentance was grounded by the Baptist, upon the approach of this kingdom, not only because it offered remission of sins, but also because judgement coincided therein with grace. He strives to affect them, first, by the mercies, and then, by the terror, of the Lord. Accordingly, he questions the Sadducees and Pharisees, who came to his baptism, the first of whom entertained no belief, and the last no fear, of the divine judgement, "who hath warned you to flee from the wrath to come?" The Holy Ghost, with which the Baptist had been filled from the womb, gave him an insight into the principles of these sectarists; and the question implies, that the baptism of John tended to deliverance, and that [p] a sense of danger was a proper motive for receiving it. It was, in fact, to those who received it, and brought forth fruits, worthy of it, a pledge of preservation from the vengeance, impending upon the Jewish people. The remark of [q] St. Peter sufficiently illustrates this point; he compares the destruction of Israel

---

[p] Mark xvi. 16. Acts ii. 40.   [q] 1 Pet. iii. 20, 21.

with that of the old world, when the family of Noah were saved by water; and then adds, "the like figure whereunto, even baptism, doth now save us."

The strength and vehemence, in the language of John, evidently denote the extremity of that wrath, which he predicted. "And now also," he cries, in a subsequent clause, "the ax is laid to the root of the trees." This denuntiation corresponded to foregoing prophecies. "Lebanon shall fall by a mighty one"—"Jerusalem shall become heaps, and the mountain of the Lord's house, as the high places of the forest"— and, "the day that cometh shall burn them up, it shall leave them neither root nor branch"—"every tree therefore, the Baptist proceeds, which bringeth not forth good fruit, ᵗ is hewn down, and cast into the fire." Their beauty had been more than once given into the hand of the enemy; but now the ax was laid to the root itself, which had hitherto escaped, and the downfall of Israel impended.

ᵗ The present tense denotes the nearness and certainty of the event. "Ἤδη κεῖται — ἐκκόπτεται — βάλλεται. See Schmid. ad. l. The first judicial act of Christ, i. e. the destruction of the Jews, and not the last Judgement of the world, seems here predicted.

This was a warning of great terror; and the Baptist appeared in "that garb of mourning, and observed" that rigour and severity of life, which were likely to enforce most deeply his prophecy of evil tidings.

It was, indeed, commonly believed, at the time, that the ruin of the Jewish state was predicted in the Scriptures; and, in the days of the Baptist, it was not supposed to be ˣ very remote. Upon this account, his words were likely to be referred by his audience to that event; and it might have been said, against the credit of his divine mission, that he only borrowed, and appropriated, the predictions of the early prophets.

But it may be argued, as it seems, upon sufficient ground, that he did not barely repeat the substance of foregoing prophecies, but really spoke from divine revelation, vouchsafed to himself.

The voice of prophecy, immediately before it ceased in Israel, denounced a day of total burning, ʸ a " great and dreadful day of the

---

ᵘ Probably, according to Macknight, the sackcloth of penitents and mourners. 1 Chron. xxi. 16.

ʷ Math. xi. 18.

ˣ " The Romans will come and take away our place and nation, John xi. 48."

ʸ Malachi iv. 5.

Lord ;"

Lord;" at the same time, intimating to the people, that universal conversion in heart, upon the preaching of Elijah, before that day of wrath, should prevent the curse from coming to smite the earth.

The woe, here denounced, had not been fulfilled, when prophecy openly revived in John. He repeated the threatening, and intimated the means of deliverance — so far Malachi and the Baptist agree. But that prophet mentions the means of deliverance in figurative and general terms; on the contrary, John uses plain language and great precision. He named the baptism of repentance for remission of sins, as the safeguard, appointed for those who would receive it. The advantage is striking on the part of the Baptist. He spoke to the same effect, as Malachi and other prophets, that wrath impended upon Israel: but he added, that his baptism was a security from it; and that, in the nature of a privilege, as well as an obligation, it set a sign upon those who received it, and placed them within that remnant, which God would spare. This particularity may appear sufficient to justify the assertion of St. Luke, that " the word of the Lord came unto John," as the repetition of a former prediction, with new and additional circumstances, if afterwards accomplished, appears a plain evidence of his prophetical character.

To strengthen the impression, which his offer of baptism might make upon his audience, he assured them, that they were entirely destitute of any other safeguard. " Think not to say within yourselves, we have Abraham to our father." Descent from this favoured patriarch was [z] the principal ground of their confidence. In pursuance of the divine promise to their great progenitor, the kingdoms of Canaan had really become the lot of their inheritance. And from this they argued, with confidence, to all the promises, made to Abraham in favour of his children. They accordingly assumed an exclusive interest in [a] all the divine blessings, and expected certain immunity from all the divine judgements, during the age of the Messias. But this notion of their hereditary privilege was declared entirely groundless; not indeed because the purpose of God was changed, and the sons of Abraham were disinherited by a repeal of

---

[z] Pocock. Miscell. pag. 172. 227.—Pugio Fidei 951.

[a] They entirely overlooked the conditional and threatning turn of the promise Exod. xix. 5. See Lightfoot. Vol. II. 533. sq.—et sup. 598. Nehem. ii. 20. Just. Mart. D. pag. 469, cited by Whitby.

the

the promise; for the language of the Baptist implies, that the blessing [b] would really descend to the children of the patriarch. But, in fact, the Jewish construction falsified the promise. It was given to the sons of Abraham, in one sense, and they, as his descendants, expected to inherit it in another. The real nature of the inheritance, and the genuine sonship to the patriarch, required in the heirs, were implied in the latitude of the promise, which was originally extended to all families of the earth. The tenor of it was, "[c] multiplying I will multiply thee;" so that one part of Abraham's blessing consisted in the infinite number of his children. Since the blessing was universal, the sonship to Abraham, on which it would devolve, must also be universal, and, consequently, could not be a natural one, as the Jews supposed. It remained therefore a question, in which all families of the earth had an equal interest, whether they had Abraham for their father in that sense, which the promise required, or only in [d] another, which it excluded. And erelong, according to the

---

[b] Luke xiii. 16. xix. 9.——Lightfoot. Vol II. 467.
[c] Heb. vi. 14.
[d] See Whitby Rom. ix. 8.

warning of the Baptist, the just distinction would be made, ^e between the true and the reputed children of the patriarch; and when the blessing descended on the genuine heirs, his natural progeny might be found to have the least interest in it, " for God is able of these stones to raise up children unto Abraham."

The language of the Baptist was evidently calculated to undeceive them, in a point of the greatest importance, which their principles misrepresented; that the promised blessing, and the sonship to Abraham, to which it was annexed, were of a spiritual nature. He taught them, that descent from the patriarch, in the ^f natural sense, afforded them no pretence, as heirs, to his blessing, which was spiritual. They might be his real and legitimate descendants, in the literal construction, and yet, at the same time, in the spiritual meaning, be no better than an evil and adulterous generation, as our Lord afterwards called them. The words of this clause are distinctly adjusted to the divine intention,

---

^e Between those who were born, of blood and of the will of man, or of the will of God. See Le Clerc. ad Hamm. ad l.
^f Rom. iv. 17. viii. 23, xi. 5. Ephes. i. 5. 1 Pet. ii. 9.

as it was afterwards explained more extensively by St. Paul, in consequence of a [g] particular revelation given to him. He [h] distinguishes, like the Baptist, between "the children of the flesh" and the "children of God," and adds, that "the children of the promise are reckoned for the seed." He further explains this point in another place, by the allegory of Hagar and Sarah; and represents [i] the son of Abraham, by the bondwoman, as cast out, because the promise was not given to the children of Abraham, merely as such; "neither [k] because they are the seed of Abraham, are they all children, but in Isaac shall thy seed be called;" that is, "they which are the children of the flesh, these are not the children of God: but the children of the promise are counted for the seed; for this is the word of promise, at this time I will come, and Sarah shall have a son."

That the inheritance of Abraham's blessing would descend, according to the election of God, and not necessarily in the natural line, was a principle before undiscovered, on which

[g] Ephes. iii. 3. sq.
[h] Compare Rom. ix. 7, 8. sq.
[i] Galat. iv. 23. sq.
[k] Compare Rom. ix. 7.

the Baptist strongly insists, not only in a declaratory, but also in a prophetical strain. For while he inculcated that construction of the promise, which would lay the inheritance open to all families of the earth, he signified that they would, in fact, be admitted to it. The one point would indeed imply the other; but it is besides enforced with an animated turn of language, "for I say unto you, that God [1] is able of these stones to raise up children unto Abraham." The clause bears a threatening cast; and although, like that of Malachi, "left I come and smite the earth with a curse," it runs conditionally, yet it relates, in the same manner, to a divine judgement impending. God has raised up other children to the patriarch, and the pretence and boast of Israel still continues, "we have Abraham to our father." It may therefore be presumed, that the divine counsel, concerning the rejection of the Jews, and the adoption of the Gentiles into the kingdom of the Messias, is predicted, in the whole clause, with as much precision, as the

---

[1] Compare Rom. xi. 23. "God is able to graft them in again." The conversions, of the Jews, and of the Gentiles, are spoken of, the one by St. Paul, and the other by the Baptist, in expressions of a similar turn. Both passages seem equally prophetical.

state of things, so early as the preaching of the Baptist, would allow. It was most probably one of those things, which the disciples of Christ, even after all their master's instructions, remained unable to bear; and the audience of John were far less likely to bear a more clear and direct declaration of this purpose of God. ——

Thus the doctrine of the Baptist appears partly designed to prepare his countrymen for the reception of a new dispensation, by combating their inveterate prejudices, and misconceptions of the law, the prophecies, and their own spiritual state. The capital points of his doctrine were directly levelled against the corruptions of the scripture-sense by the Jews. Discarding the moral law, they rested in ritual righteousness, as a state of salvation; and arrogated to themselves the blessing of Abraham's children, by virtue of lineal descent from him; and, in order to accommodate the kingdom of the Messias to their principles, they represented it to be a state of temporal greatness, and [m] temporal blessings. The system of their opinions was uniform, and adjusted in all its parts; but when the Baptist declared that the kingdom

[m] Matth. xx. 20.

of the Meſſias, the true righteouſneſs, the promiſe itſelf, and the genuine fonſhip to Abraham, were all ſpiritual, he overturned the whole. And ſince, in the execution of his purpoſe, he difcloſed the ſpiritual nature, and characteriſtical principles of the kingdom of heaven, then ready to appear, and denounced the impending rejection and ruin of Iſrael, and the adoption of other children, as heirs of Abraham's bleſſing, his baptifmal doctrine appears, not ſimply admonitory, but evidently prophetical, and ſtrictly ſuited to prepare the way for the ſpiritual kingdom of the Meſſias, by pointing out, and removing, impediments to the reception of it.——

The following reflection ariſes from the general ſubſtance of the foregoing obſervations. Many expreſſions, in the Jewiſh Scriptures, depreciated the law, and ſome implied the abolition of it. The force of all theſe was felt; and to palliate and pervert them, had generally been the favourite ſtudy of the ſcribes and teachers of Iſrael. To ingenuity and learning, exerted to defend the law, their zeal added the authority of the great council. Accordingly, the attempt to change, and much more to ſuperſede, the law, was marked as an inſuperable obſtacle to the
admiſſion

admission of any one, who laid claim to a prophetical character; it prevented all question, respecting the truth of his pretensions, and death was to be inflicted upon him, as a convicted impostor.—Yet, neither the popular construction of Scripture, nor even the judicial interdiction, had any influence with the Baptist. From whence it appears, that he proceeded by " necessity laid upon him," that is, by divine command, to recall and authorize that genuine sense of promise and prophecy, which was not received in Israel. For the essential principles of the human mind, by which it resolves and operates in all conjunctures, render it incredible, that he would have thus exposed himself to rejection and death, if he knew that he was a false prophet; and it must have been impossible for him to execute his baptismal ministry, in such a strain of prediction, if he had not been a true one.

SERMON III.

MARK i. 7.

There cometh One, Mightier than I, after me.

THAT part of the baptismal doctrine, already considered, consisted of admonition and prophecy. The first, was applied to correct the spiritual mistakes and haughtiness of the Jews; and the last, tended to shew that the kingdom of Messias, was of such a nature and character, that it required in those, who desired to enter therein, a state of mind and principles, entirely contrary to the prevalent disposition of Israel. Upon the whole, the Baptist gave full assurance to his hearers, that, unless they would return to God, by the baptism of water, entirely discarding their prejudices and presumption,

sumption, and impressed with a just and repentant sense of their sinful and unforgiven state, the blessings, which God had promised to the children of Abraham, would be inherited by others, but rejection and ruin impended upon them. He disclosed the divine counsel to save them, if they would embrace it; and, at the same time, predicted the wrath, which God had determined against them, if they refused it. And, as the discharge of his baptismal office, so far, immediately tended " to prepare the way of the Lord," and, " to make ready a people" to receive him, " what shall we do then," was a very interesting question; and such as the tenor of his doctrine might have been expected to suggest, not only to some, but to all, that heard it.

But there was another, and that a more considerable part of his office. He " verily baptized with the baptism of repentance;" but not without continually " saying unto the people, that they should believe on him, which should come after;" and, as this was the principal drift of his preaching, it is represented by St. Mark, as the substance of it;

SERMON III.

it; "John preached, saying, there cometh One, mightier than I, after me."

That it may appear how he proceeded to excite and support that faith in the Messias, which he represented, as an indispensable qualification for admission to his kingdom, it will be my present endeavour, to shew in what terms, and to what effect, he spake of the Messias, during that time, wherein he continued unknown to him. For this purpose, I return to the baptismal doctrine, as it stands in the text of St. Matthew, and go on with it from that clause, where I left it at the close of the last discourse.

What the Baptist had already preached, whether it respected the religious corruptions of the Jews, and their rejection from the Messiah's kingdom, and the adoption of the Gentiles, in their place, or the spiritual character of the approaching dispensation, and the terms of admission to it; was delivered with such prophetical discernment and fervency, as evidently to imply, that he acted under the informing and animating influence of the Holy Ghost.

He next proceeds to speak directly of the Messias, and to characterize his office, and to disclose some of his attributes.

He first inculcates the subordinate character, and limited effect, of his ministry, "I indeed baptize you with water unto repentance," implying the great superiority of the Messiah's baptism to his own. Through the whole verse, the baptism of water, and the weakness of John, seem to be put in contrast to the baptism of the Holy Ghost, and the power of the Messias, with an intent to justify that attribute, which intervenes, "he that cometh after me, is mightier than I."

The Messias is here represented in that light, wherein the public exercise of his office would shortly place him; and the attribute relates not to one only, of all his mighty works, as singly opposed to the baptism of John; but comprehends that general demonstration of power, which, according to the prophecies, and the common expectation of the Jewish people, would be displayed in the ministry of the Messias. It stands also in the stronger light, on account of the comparative form, "a mightier than I cometh;" for while John preached, "the kingdom of heaven is at hand," he did no miracle; but, on the contrary, the Messias argued, "if I, by the finger of God, cast out devils, no doubt the kingdom of God is come

come unto you." The voice of John, " crying in the wilderness, prepare ye the way of the Lord," proclaimed his approach; and the Baptist afterwards bore testimony to his person. But, of his actual presence, his own signs and wonders were greater witness, than that of John. The attribute of power was therefore suited to give the most signal and majestic representation of his ministry.

The Baptist proceeds — " whose shoes I am not worthy to bear." St. Luke, in the parallel passage, explains, and even exaggerates, that comparative self-abasement, which the words of John convey. They place, in a striking point of view, that great humility, which distinguished his own character, and aggrandize, to the highest degree, him that was to come. Other divine messengers, whether of human or [a] angelic natures, speak of each other and of themselves, as brethren and fellow-servants; but the strength of this expression, considered as tending to exalt one prophet above another, is entirely singular in Scripture.

In these clauses, the Baptist disclosed two very signal attributes of the Messias, his mighty power and transcendent dignity.

[a] Revel. xix. 10. xxii. 9.

Herein indeed he delivered nothing, that contradicted the notions of his audience. They had reasoned from the prophecies, to a similar effect; and as their expectation, that the Messias would be incomparable in power and greatness, was grounded upon the predictions of their own Scriptures; it was not impossible, that the Baptist's knowledge of both these attributes, might rather appear to be derived from antecedent prophecy, than from the revelation of the Holy Spirit to himself; and, upon that account, might seem to afford no unquestionable evidence of his mission from God.

In order to shew, that John characterized the Messiah by these attributes, in consequence of divine inspiration, particularly vouchsafed to himself; it might be observed, that his construction of the prophecies, which relate to the Messiah, greatly surpassed the Jewish interpretation of them, and unfolded their genuine sense, which was either not discovered, or not received, in Israel.

But, without enlarging upon this evidence of the reality of his prophetical character, it may perhaps here, as in a former case, be shewn from the clause, under immediate
con-

SERMON III. 53

consideration, that both attributes, here ascribed to the Messiah by the Baptist, had been dictated by divine revelation, particularly given to him.

He contrasts the baptism of the Holy Ghost to that of water. No construction of Scripture seems to have raised any expectation, that can be assuredly traced, in Israel, of a baptism by water, that would entirely overrule the principles and law of the Jews. A master of Israel knew it not; and much less would the people apprehend and expect the baptism of the Holy Ghost, to complete what the baptism of water began.

They believed indeed, that the Holy Spirit, which departed from Israel, on the death of Malachi, would return, in the days of the Messias. But this expectation, however just, was grounded upon a general and loose construction of the prophecies, that the Spirit would be poured out in the latter days.

But the turn, which the Baptist has given to these prophecies, goes farther than barely to foretell the restoration of the Spirit to Israel. He has not only shewn with what strictness, the language of the prophets had been adjusted to the divine intention; but has even enlarged upon their prophecies, by the addition of new and original circumstances.

He evidently seems acquainted with the [a] divine intention, to accomplish in the heart, by the washing of the Holy Ghost, what the washing of water should previously perform for the body. Accordingly, he represents his external baptism of water, as the preparatory sign, but the inward baptism of the Spirit, as the perfect accomplishment. A close relation [b] and analogy had been fixed between them, and, according to the apparent import of the words of John, would erelong be exemplified in the approaching dispensation. When therefore he laid together the two baptisms, of water, and of the Holy Ghost, he virtually disclosed the real design of God, to connect the washing of water, as the sign, with the washing of the Holy Ghost, as the thing signified, in a gospel Sacrament; and gave a reason, till then undiscovered, for his directing the prophets to characterize [c] the return of the Spirit,

---

[a] All that was internal in baptism was ἐπυράνιον. John iii. 12.——See Whit'y on Ephes. i. 3.
[b] Titus iii. 5. James i. 8. Mede Opp. 62.
[c] Thus, but much more expressively, Jesus afterwards, under the image of living water, described the efficacy of spiritual grace. John iv. 14.——Isaiah xliv. 3. of which see the

Targ.

with his gifts and operations, by the baptismal element of water.

Another confiderable addition to the prophecies, concerning the return of the Spirit, was made by the Baptift, when he attributed the reftoration of it to the Meffias. For, as this fuperior baptifm, and that of water, are contradiftinguifhed, fo alfo are the minifters of each; and John ftates the fimilarity and the difference between them, and afcribes the baptifm of the Holy Ghoft, as truly and properly to the Meffiah, as the other to himfelf. All that was external and imperfect in baptifm, he confines to that of water, and to himfelf, the minifter of it; but what would be effectually wrought in the heart, he attributes to the baptifm of the Spirit, and to the power of him, that came after himfelf. He feems alfo to reprefent it, as a mighty work, that would evidently afcertain the tranfcen-

---

Targ. Expof. quoted by Whitby John vii. 39.——See alfo Wolf. ibid.——Ifai. lviii. 7, et Surenhufii Catallag. 358, 360.——Ezek. xxxvi. 25. Zechar. xiv. 8.—Reland. Palæftin. 352. Cocceius Opp. Tom. VI, in calce, Ep. 76.

dent dignity, as well as ^c power, of him, to whom he afcribed it.

The Baptift feems to have made another addition to the prophecies, refpecting the reftoration of the Holy Spirit to Ifrael. For the words, " and ^d with fire," feem to be put in contraft to thofe, in which John had mentioned the baptifmal element ufed by himfelf; and, upon that account, appear to carry the fame fpecial reference to the manner of accomplifhing the baptifm of the Holy Ghoft, by the Meffias, which the water bears to the manner of adminiftering the inferior baptifm of John.

To confirm this fuppofition, it may be obferved, that the baptifm of the Holy Ghoft was actually accomplifhed, by the Meffias, with fuch appearances, as the words, " with fire," would manifeftly denote.

It may be further obferved, that, on many occafions, ^e fire had been employed, as the

---

^c John xiv. 12. See Tillotf. Serm. 143.
^d Of the genuinenefs of thefe words, fee Mill. ad l. et Le Clerc. Epift. ad Optimianum. Bibl. Select. Wolf. ad l.
^e Fire was the ufual fymbol of the divine prefence. Gen. xv. 17. xxiv. 17. xl. 38. — Numb. ix. 15. — Deuteron. iv. 33. Jortin. Rem. Eccl. H. Vol. III. p. 392. fq. Jeffery's Tracts, V. II. p. 408.

fenfible

sensible sign of the divine presence. As the God of Abraham manifested himself in a flaming fire, when he authorized Moses to deliver his peculiar people from Egyptian bondage, and to bring them into covenant with Jehovah, as their king; so again he manifested himself, by the same symbol, when he empowered the Apostles, to rescue the world from spiritual bondage, and to introduce them into the kingdom of the Messiah.

There seems then a reasonable ground for that literal interpretation of the words, " and with fire," which many expositors of this passage have adopted; and upon that footing, the Baptist has delivered, in this clause, an evident and original prophecy.

These several circumstances, immediately preceding, when laid together, are sufficient, it is presumed, to shew, that when John assigned transcendent power and dignity, and the baptism of the Holy Ghost, to the Messias, his doctrine in all those respects, however conformable it might be to foregoing prophecies, was nevertheless the result of divine revelation, directly vouchsafed to himself.

To proceed, — The Baptist, having thus attributed to the Messias the administration of baptism with the Holy Ghost, represents him, in the subsequent clause, under another character; " whose fan is in his hand, and he will thoroughly purge his floor, and gather his wheat into the garner, but he will burn up the chaff with unquenchable fire."

The import of these expressions may be determined by their sense in former prophecies.

" I will fan them, with a fan, — I will destroy my people," saith the Lord by [f] Jeremiah; and again, " I will send unto Babylon fanners, that shall fan her, and shall empty her land; for in the day of trouble they shall be against her round about;" — and Israel, under captivity, is called [g] the Lord's " threshing," and " the son of his floor;" and [h] wheat and chaff are very frequently opposed to each other in Scripture, and in a sense sufficiently obvious.

[f] Jerem. xv. 7. xli. 16. li. 2. Compare Amos ix. 9. Luke xxii. 31.
[g] Isaiah xxi. 10.—See Glass. Rhetor. Sac. 303, 304.
[h] Psalm i. 4.—Job xxi. 18.—Jerem. xx. 28.—

The

The meaning of the clause therefore appears to be this; he will discriminate, and that thoroughly, the good corn from the unprofitable produce, in his husbandry, and gather the one, but destroy the other.

The Messiah is here represented in a judicial character, as in a foregoing clause; but not, as it seems, in relation only to the same act of judgement, which the Baptist had already attributed to him. For, this passage appears to contain a prediction of farther extent, than the former; and although it may relate, in a primary sense, to the rejection and ruin of Israel, and the admission of the Gentiles, in their place, to the Messiah's kingdom; yet it may be understood, in an ultimate sense, of the universal act of his judicial power, the judgement of the last day.

A comparison of the expressions, in both passages, may perhaps tend to illustrate and confirm this point. " Now the axe is laid unto the [i] root of the trees; every tree therefore, that bringeth not forth good fruit, is hewn down, and cast into the fire." The present tense, which runs through the verse,

---

[i] Deus minatur—fœderis sui derelictionem, quod est velut arborem radicitus exscindere. Grot. ad l.

according to the opinion of an [k] able critic on the original text, implies the certainty and near approach of the vengeance denounced; and upon comparing this prophecy with others, [l] strictly parallel, in the old Testament, it may seem most probable, that the ruin of the Jewish state and people, is alone predicted in it.

But this clause has a different tenor. Οὗ τὸ πίυον ἐν τῇ χειρὶ αὐτῦ — if the verb be supplied, in the same tense, which runs through the rest of the verse, it must be rendered, " whose fan will be in his hand, and he will thoroughly purge his floor, and will gather his wheat into the garner, but will burn up the chaff with unquenchable fire."

If this be allowed, our view will not be so immediately confined, as it was in the former clause, to one, and that an imminent, act of the Messiah's judicial power; but may be carried forward to [m] another, and a more remote, exercise of it.

---

[k] Schmid. ad. l.

[l] Isaiah x. 33, 34.—Micah iii. 12.

[m] Posteriora hujus commatis verba, de colligendis frugibus et comburendis paleis, ad ultimi judicii dien pertinent, ut apparet ex collatione verb. Christi infra xiii. 30. 49. —— Grot. ad l.

If to this it be added, that he shall purge his floor, "thoroughly," διακαθαριεῖ, and not in a limited manner, the act intended may seem, not national only, but universal; and, since the fire of his vengeance is called "unquenchable," the judgement, to which the clause relates, may appear final and irreversible. On these accounts then, the passage may be imagined to have a farther view, than barely to the destruction of the holy city, and the rejection of the Jews; both of which events, as the prophecies of Christ, and St. Paul, seem to intimate, will expire when the times of the Gentiles shall be fulfilled.

Upon the whole, the clause, under immediate consideration, apparently surpasses the former, and contains a more enlarged prediction. The foregoing prophecy respected the ruin of Israel solely; the latter, has possibly the same relation, in a primary meaning, but at the same time extends, in an ultimate sense, to the Messiah's judgement of all the world. And perhaps the prophecy, which Christ himself afterwards delivered, of his approaching vengeance upon Israel, had the same respect to his real and personal coming to inflict final punishment upon all his enemies.

There

There is also another material difference between the two passages. The Baptist had before declared that vengeance impended upon Israel; he now not only denounces it to all the adversaries of the Messias, but also represents it as inflicted by him; the fan and the floor are his, as Lord of the harvest; he will gather and he will burn.

Thus also the writer to the Hebrews ascribes to the Messiah, as his proper and personal prerogative, an infallible and irreversible judgement, and the infliction of vengeance. For he had, as a son, the administration of all things over his own house, and, as such, had promised a rest to the faithful; but to them, who grieved him with their unbelief, he said in his wrath, "they shall not enter into my rest." In this chapter to the Hebrews, and in the clauses of the baptismal doctrine, now under consideration, admission to the kingdom of God, and exclusion from it, are represented as dependent upon the [n] Messiah, as Judge of all. ——

Here St. Matthew finishes the account of the baptismal doctrine of John, before the coming of Jesus to Jordan. St. Luke adds,

[n] Heb. iii. 8. 19.

" and

"and many other things, in his exhortation, preached he unto the people." But if that Evangelist had not already given the substance of them, he probably would have extended the account. It may therefore be presumed, that what has been already considered, forms a just compendium of the baptismal doctrine, delivered in that interval, however the Baptist might enlarge and illustrate it, upon frequent calls to repeat it.

He has displayed the character of the Messiah, by four capital attributes; by his mighty power; by his transcendent dignity; by his baptism with the Holy Ghost, as a Priest; and by his judicial authority, as a King, to be exercised erelong over Israel, and finally over the whole world. And from the amount of the baptismal doctrine, hitherto considered, it appears, that his knowledge, of the nature and purpose of the Gospel, and of the attributes and offices of the Messias, far exceeded that of the Apostles, till the same divine Spirit, which instructed and guided the Baptist, had also shed his influence upon them.

After

After this illustration of the prophetical testimony of John to the Messias, I proceed, in the last place, to shew, that it was delivered, while he remained unknown to the Baptist.

Before John had attained that age, ° which the law appointed for entering upon a priestly function, it may be reasonably presumed, that he did not receive a command to baptize, and knew not the substance of the doctrine, which he afterwards delivered. "He was in the wilderness, till the day of his shewing unto Israel;" there it was, that the word of the Lord came unto him; and, in pursuance of that divine mission, he began to exercise his office ᵖ there, whilst Jesus continued ᑫ at Nazareth in Galilee.

After the Baptist had preached in the hill-country of the wilderness of Judæa, near to Hebron, the supposed place of his nativity, and education, he came into the region ʳ about Jordan, where Jerusalem, and ˢ all Judæa, went out to him, and were baptized.

° Numb iv. 3.—1 Chron. xxiii. 3.
ᵖ What went ye out into the wilderness to see? Luke vii. 24.
ᑫ Matth. ii. 23, compared with iii. 1.
ʳ Luke iii. 4.   ˢ Matth. iii. 5.

Faith

SERMON III.

Faith in the Messias, then speedily coming to his kingdom, was the ᵗ capital article of his baptismal exhortations; and it has been already shewn, by what doctrines he endeavoured to remove impediments to his reception, and by what characters and attributes he described him. As these attributes seem to be all, which John assigned to the Messias, before he had baptized him, perhaps it may be allowable to infer, that no other had been, as yet, revealed to the Baptist. He was called and commissioned to manifest the Messias unto Israel; and, with a view to the accomplishment of this office, he was instructed to represent him, as far superior to himself in power and dignity, and to ascribe to him the prerogative of baptizing with the Holy Ghost, and of immediately exercising judgement upon Israel, and finally upon the whole world; and he had been informed, that the person, upon whom he should see the Spirit descend and remain, was the same, that should baptize with the Holy Ghost.

These attributes of the Messiah, and, as it seems, these alone, having been revealed

ᵗ Mark i. 7.

to John, either by the word of the Lord, at his mission, or by the Holy Ghost, since his original call, he baptized in the wide and populous district abovementioned, from the time of his first receiving the divine commission, till the Messias met him at the river Jordan. This necessarily must have been a period of considerable length; and according to the gospel-writers, it was an interval of six months. The baptismal doctrine, which he delivered during the whole of this period, seems to afford no evidences, that he had received any more extensive and particular information, concerning the Messiah, or his offices, than what the above abstract contains.

From appearances therefore it may be presumed, that divine revelation had not, as yet, acquainted him, who was the Messiah; and as this presumption seems to be confirmed by his express assertion, " I knew him not," it will be attempted, in the remainder of this discourse, to fix the sense of it, and the time, to which it must be restrained.

If he is supposed to disclaim, a knowledge of the Messiah's person; then the expression of the Evangelist, " [u] he was in the desarts, till the day of his shewing unto Israel," must be taken strictly, as overruling

[u] Luke i. 80.

any supposition, that the Baptist visited Jerulem, at festival-seasons, according to the direction of the law, with which Jesus of Nazareth complied. And it seems extremely probable, that John did not conform to this legal injunction, and that the Evangelist really intended to obviate any belief that he obeyed it. For it may be observed, that John was set apart for the baptismal office, and filled with the Holy Ghost, from his mother's womb. He might therefore all along be guided to hold himself independent of legal obligations. This would not be without precedent in the case of Elias, the declared type of the Baptist. While the law confined the sacrifical acts of religion to the Temple, and the Temple-ministers, he held a public sacrifice on the top of [w] Carmel. And, as the type is always inferior to the antitype, and John was continually filled with the Spirit, the same divine direction, under which Elias had acted, may be supposed to have discharged the Baptist also from the restriction of the Law. The diligence and nicety, observed by the Evangelists, in their relation of particulars, appears of great weight in this question. Their

---

[w] 1 King. xviii. 19.

account is this: that "the call of John happened " in the wildernefs," and that he preached there firft, and then came, and baptized, " in all the region round about Jordan,"—and that, after fix months, Jefus came from Nazareth in Galilee, ʷ beyond Jerufalem and Samaria, and met the Baptift at Jordan. As this accurate detail, of the gradual circumftances, feems the natural refult of an ˣ intention to reprefent Jefus of Nazareth, and John, as perfonally unknown to each other, the affertion of the Baptift, "I knew him not," may reafonably be underftood to imply, that he knew not the perfon of Jefus.

But it may alfo be taken in a fenfe, equivalent to that of a fimilar expreffion of Jefus concerning John," they knew him not," which relates not to the perfon, but the divine character, of the Baptift. In perfon, as the Baptift, John was clearly known; but he was not received as that Elias, which was for to come. In the fame fenfe, John might

---

ᵘ Lightfoot, Vol. II. p. 755.
ʷ Samaria lay between; and the journey from Galilee that way to Jerufalem, would take up three days. Jofeph. in vit. et Antiq. L. 2. C. 5. See Lightfoot Harmony, 3d part, p. 605.
ˣ Compare Luke ii. 51. Matth. xiii. 55. Mark vi. 33.

profess, he knew not that Jesus was the Messiah; and this construction of his words may perhaps be confirmed by the following considerations.

The substance of his preaching, before the Messias appeared, was this; "there cometh one, mightier than I." He was sufficiently qualified for delivering such a notice, if he had been assured, on divine authority, that the mighty one would speedily appear; and supposing him to have known, who it was, that should bear this great character, the intelligence was apparently of no present use, as this stage of his office did not require it. He was qualified both as a prophet, and a forerunner, without it; and God usually reveals all, that is necessary, but nothing premature or superfluous. As therefore no evidences have occurred in the baptismal doctrine, hitherto considered, that John really knew Jesus of Nazareth to be the Messias, it seems a reasonable inference, that some few of his attributes had been revealed to the Baptist, but no determinate indication given, that Jesus was the mighty one, whose coming he had predicted.

When the absolute appearance of the Messias required that he should be manifested to Israel,

Israel, in the fullest latitude, then indeed it would become indispensably necessary, that the Baptist should know him, in his divine character; but it was not immediately requisite, before the opportunity arrived of shewing him personally to the people. Upon this footing then, the whole of that knowledge, which had been imparted to John, either at his call, or since, was strictly adjusted to the nature of his office, as forerunner; and extended no further, than to qualify him for that part of his ministry, which has been hitherto considered.

As to the time, to which the words of the Baptist, " I knew him not," extend; if they are taken in the first of the two senses abovementioned, it comprehends nearly the whole of his life; if they are understood in the latter sense, the period, to which they relate, commences with his call to the baptismal ministry; but in either case, expires upon the coming of Jesus to his baptism. And perhaps the greatest strength of the assertion, may lie in this latter sense, and in this reference of it to a period, posterior to the commencement of his baptismal ministry.

The case then appears to stand thus; it may be presumed, that John could not know
the

SERMON III.

the Messias, without a divine revelation; and the substance of his doctrine, as the Evangelists deliver it, during his ministry of half a year, gives no evidence, that he knew the Messias, during that period; and consequently, it seems to be credible, that he applied the assertion, " I knew him not," in that sense, and to that interval of time. Upon the whole, there appears a sufficient reason to imagine, that the Baptist intended to assert, that he knew not the person of Jesus, and also, that revelation had never acquainted him, who was the Messias, before they met at the river Jordan; so that, in fact, he had predicted the immediate coming of the Messias, and disclosed some of his attributes, by virtue of one revelation, but, at the same time, was left unable to know him, whenever he should appear, without another.

SERMON IV.

JOHN i. 6, 7.

There was a man, sent from God, whose name was John — the same came for a witness —

ALL the characters of the Messias, which have been hitherto considered, were ascribed to him, before the coming of Jesus to Jordan; and the Baptist seems to have disclaimed any knowledge of him, previous to that interview, either as to his person, or his office. Some reasons were offered, at the conclusion of the former discourse, for interpreting the assertion, "I knew him not," in both these senses; and in the last of them, it was then applied to all that period of his baptismal ministry, in which he continued strictly the forerunner. For

the

the Baptist, considered as only the prophet of the Highest, might have been sufficiently qualified to prepare his way, without knowing him, either as to his person, or his divine character, that is, without knowing Jesus of Nazareth, as such, or that He was the Messiah.

But there is another light, in which the last only of the Evangelists seems to have represented the Baptist. He "came for a witness," as well as a prophet; and it appears requisite to distinguish and separate these characters, since the assertion, " I knew him not," cannot extend to them equally, and be applied, with the same propriety, to the one, as to the other; which will be shewn more fully, as I proceed. ⎯

As this discourse will treat of the testimony of John, immediately subsequent to that interview, wherein the Messias became known to him; and as that testimony was grounded principally upon the baptism of Jesus, it will be proper to begin with a view of that important transaction.

" Jesus came from Nazareth of Galilee to Jordan unto John, to be baptized of him — but John forbad him —"

[z] Matth. iii. 13, and Mark i. 9.

As the Messias now confessedly appeared, he not only ascertained the divine mission of John, as his forerunner, by thus fullfilling the principal prophecy, which he had delivered, but also opened to the Baptist a new and distinct part of his office. Upon this interview, John ceased to be simply the forerunner; and it became incumbent upon him, in future, to bear testimony that the mighty one, whose way he had prepared, and whose immediate coming he had predicted, was really come, and had manifested himself openly.

If therefore it be considered, that the circumstances and office of John, were thus altered, by the appearance of the Messias at Jordan, the case may possibly seem to require that his assertion, " I knew him not," should be extended, as far as this interview, but not beyond it. For, although the person of the Messias had not been revealed to the Baptist, before this meeting, as the tenor of his baptismal doctrine, and that direct assertion, if it has been rightly interpreted, seem to imply; yet, from his conduct, during this interview, it may be justly concluded, that the Messias was made known to him then, by immediate revelation.

Instances

Inſtances occur in Scripture, which cloſely reſemble the preſent caſe. "[a] The Lord had told Samuel in his ear, to morrow I will ſend thee a man; and thou ſhalt anoint him to be captain over my people Iſrael, that he may ſave my people out of the hand of the Philiſtines. And when Samuel ſaw Saul, the Lord ſaid unto him, behold the man whom I told thee of; this ſame ſhall reign over my people."

[b] The ſame prophet received another commiſſion, reſpecting the ſucceſſor of Saul. The Lord ſaid unto him; "I will ſend thee to Jeſſe, the Bethlehemite, for I have provided me a king among his ſons. Call Jeſſe to the ſacrifice, and I will ſhew thee what thou ſhalt do; and thou ſhalt anoint unto me, him whom I name unto thee" When David appeared, "the Lord ſaid, ariſe, anoint him, for this is he."

Theſe paſſages are here produced at length, that the parallel between the caſe of Samuel, and that of John, may ſtand in the ſtrongeſt light. The prophet, on both thoſe occaſions, received a commiſſion to anoint the future king; yet then, and in the whole of the in-

---

[a] 1 Sam. ix. 15.   [b] 1 Sam. xvi. 11, 12.

terval, which preceded his appearance, Samuel knew him not; but when the king stood before him, the prophet instantly knew him by another revelation; and the case appears to be the same with the Baptist in both respects.

That John knew the divine character of Jesus, seems to be ascertained by his conduct upon this occasion, as it marks in the most lively and affecting colours, his deep veneration of the incomparable person, then before him. He came to be baptized; but John forbad him; in the language of humility and awe, but not of authoritative refusal. His own spiritual necessities, as they lay deep in his mind, were immediate on his tongue; "I have need to be baptized of thee." He made that profession of faith in him, who would baptize with the Holy Ghost, which his own baptismal doctrine had constantly enforced upon others. Like them, he needed the baptism of the Spirit; and felt his great unworthiness to baptize his, as well as

---

^c In the last of these two instances, the prophet called all the Sons of Jesse to the sacrifice, not knowing which of them the Lord had chosen—after Eliab, the rest of them passed successively before Samuel, and he said unto Jesse "the Lord hath not chosen these." Revelation gave no direction, respecting any of these — but when the youngest of all came in, the Lord said immediately, "this is he."

their,

their, Mighty Superior; "Comeft thou to me?"— His hefitation incurred not the flighteft rebuke; it turned entirely upon the fenfe of his own extreme inferiority. The great perfon, then before him, faw it's principle, and overruled it, in the gentleft manner; "fuffer it to be fo now, for thus it becometh us to fulfil all [d] righteoufnefs." From the turn of this paffage, it feems that Jefus fpake with a particular view, to the circumftances of himfelf and the Baptift, at the time, with refpect to their feveral offices — as if he had faid more at large; that his hour of baptizing with the Holy Ghoft, to which John had alluded, was not yet arrived; although that, with every other mighty work, affigned to him, would be accomplifhed in their appointed feafon; but, in the mean while, that his miniftry was to begin here, and in this manner — "Then he fuffered him."

From this interefting conference, it may

---

[d] Plato, cited by Schultetus. Exercit. Evang. ad l. δικαιοσύνη ἐςιν τὰ ἑαυτῦ πράτlειν, κỳ μὴ πολυπραγμονεῖν. *Juftitia eft, facere quæ fui funt muneris, et non curiofum effe in negotiis alienis. Æquum igitur Chriftus judicat, ut Johannes juftitiam fuam, ipfe fuam, impleat; hoc eft, ut demandato fibi munere uterque defungatur.*

be

be possible to define, with greater precision than before, the substance and extent of divine revelation, respecting the Messias, hitherto vouchsafed to John. For thence it appears, first, that the Baptist had not been, as yet, acquainted, at what time and upon what occasion, he should see the Spirit of God descend upon the Messias; or even that he should actually receive the baptism of water. If John, had been apprized, that, on the baptism of the Messias, the Spirit would visibly descend upon him, or even that it was in the divine intention, that he should baptize him; all hesitation, on his part, from whatever principle of comparative self-abasement it might arise, would have been antecedently overruled. He would most probably have hasted to the accomplishment of his office, in this point, as it would authenticate the divine mission of Jesus and his own, rather than have delayed it by the smallest reluctance. As this then appears a new example, that divine revelation had not hitherto fully informed the Baptist, in all points, that respected the Messias, and even his own ministry; it may help to confirm an inference, already made, that the particular

person

[e] person of the Messias had not been revealed to him, at his original mission.

But it is more material to observe, from this transaction, that Jesus evidently dictated to John the counsel of God concerning his own baptism. The Holy Ghost, with which the Baptist had been filled from the womb, appears here to have given him no direction. The words of Jesus, were left to supply the place of the Spirit's influence; and the authority and inspiration of Jesus, even before he was anointed with the Spirit, were, in fact, attested by John, when he obeyed his requisition, in a case, wherein revelation from God had not previously instructed him, and wherein also his own mind had suggested an opposite conduct.

Since then, according to the foregoing circumstances, the Baptist apparently knew that the Messias then stood before him, he could not, it may be presumed, baptize him, as a disciple. For, in whatever points, the baptism of water was accommodated to the converts of John, in all of them, it was evidently unsuitable to the Messias. Jesus therefore must have received it upon some

---

[e] See the close of the last discourse.

SERMON IV.

other principle; and the Scripture seems to indicate, that he was publickly ᶠ consecrated to the priesthood of the Gospel, by baptism, as the ᵍ priests of the law were ushered into their ministry, by the washing of water. He became subject to the law for man; and ʰ in all things it behoved him to be made like unto his brethren, that he might be, not only a merciful, but also a faithful, high priest, in things pertaining to God, to make reconciliation for the sins of the people.

To proceed — This inaugural ceremony was scarcely concluded, when ⁱ the heavens were opened, and the Spirit of God descended, in a bodily shape, and, in the sight of John, and of the surrounding multitude, ᵏ rested upon Jesus. He was thus " ˡ anointed with the Holy Ghost, and with power;" and through the whole of his ministry upon

---

ᶠ According to prophecy; Psalm xlv. 7. Isai. lxi. 1.

ᵍ Exod. xxix. 4. 7. Levit. viii. 6. See Lightfoot, Vol. II. 476.

ʰ Hebr. ii. 17.

ᵏ Isaiah xi. 2. — Abarbanel, on this place observes, that the *resting* of the Spirit upon the Messiah, was one of his prerogatives.

ˡ Acts x. 38. — The substance of that commission, which this unction gave him, is recited by himself, in the words of Isaiah, Luke iv. 18, 19.

F   earth,

earth, his miracles were wrought, his doctrines and prophecies were delivered, by virtue of that Spirit, which at this time descended and remained upon him. The voice of the Father immediately followed, " ᵐ this is my beloved Son, in whom I am well-pleased." In fact, this was the baptismal form of the Messias; for by the title of his beloved Son, the Father ⁿ glorified Jesus to be an high-priest, and, at the same time, declared the sufficiency and success of his sacerdotal ministry, " in thee I am ᵒ well-

---

ᵐ Mark i. 11. Luke iii. 22, &c.—Quod alius dicit, in quo mihi complacui; alius, in te complacui; alius in te complacuit mihi; si quæris quid horum in illâ voce sonuerit, quodlibet accipe, dummodo intelligas eos, qui non eandem locutionem retulerunt, eandem retulisse sententiam. August. Lib. 2. de Conf. Evang. c. 14.

ⁿ Compare 2 Pet. i. 17. sq. where The Voice of the Father is urged as a powerful testimony to Jesus; and to this Voice he himself probably refers, John v. 37. See Macknight on Har. §. 142. τον λογον αυτȣ ȣκ εχετε μενοντα εν ὑμιν, that is, ye have not retained in your minds his word, when he bore witness of me, from heaven. Compare Heb. ii. 1. προσεχειν τοις ἀκȣσθεισι is equivalent to λογον εχειν μενοντα, and παραρρυειν, to the contrary.

ᵒ See Budæus Comm. Ling. Gr. 316. Schmid. ad l. Chemnitius thinks, that St. Paul alludes to this Voice of the Father. Coloss. i. 19. Of the original word, which the Seventy render by ευδοκια, frequent use is made, when God is said to receive a sacrifice favourably, or not. Levit. xix. 7. xxii. 23, 27. Psalm li. 19. Isaiah liii. 10. " the pleasure of the Lord shall prosper in his hand." The Chald. Par. on this Chap. says, that it was the good pleasure of the Lord to forgive all sins for his (the Messiah's) sake; that so they might see the kingdom of the Messias.
                                                                Braun.

pleased." The doctrine of the Apostles fully illustrates this last expression. According to them, the source of human salvation, and of all spiritual blessings, is εὐδοκία Θεῦ, the good pleasure of his will in Christ. The Redeemer himself therefore professes to the Father; "in burnt-offerings and sacrifices for sin thou hast had no pleasure—lo, I come, to do thy will, O God;"—and by this will we are sanctified, through the offering of that body, which God had prepared for the Messias, and the Father hath made us accepted in the Beloved. He pleased the Father, and thereby prevailed with him, in behalf of men, because he was the Son of God; and to this construction the passage, as it was pronounced by the Father, appears immediately to lead; but the contrary opinion, that, because he had pleased the Father, he became the Son of God, reverses the tenor, and seems to destroy the force, of the sentence.

[p] Immediately, that is, probably, before

Braun. ad Hebr. p. 627, et Selecta Sacr. pag. 358. Hence the Messiah's ministry is called the "acceptable year" of the Lord, and the Lord is said to have, or not to have, "pleasure" in sacrifice. Ephes. i. 5. Heb. x. 6.

[p] Mark i. 12.

sufficient time had been given to the Baptist, for pointing out Jesus, as the Messias, to the people, the Spirit led him up into the wilderness, to undergo the temptation. But as John was now enabled to enlarge his baptismal doctrine very considerably, in consequence of the Messiah's actual appearance; he accordingly referred to it in his first testimony, subsequent to the baptism of Jesus. He declared to the multitude, who had been, either actually present at this miraculous transaction, or, at least, made acquainted with it; "[q] this was he, of whom I spake, he that cometh after me, is preferred before me, for he was before me." This designation of the Messias, is nearly, although not absolutely, personal; and the Baptist apparently speaks, of one, who had been lately present, and to persons, who then had seen him. ——

The attribute, which is contained in the words, "he was before me," is a new ground of dignity, and surpasses any character of the Messias, which John had mentioned, before the baptism of Jesus. This seems therefore another example, that the character of the Messias was only gradually unfolded to the

[q] John i. 15.

Baptist.

Baptist. It likewise appears from hence, that the Holy Ghost, which had notified the person of the Messias to John, suggested also this eminent attribute of his preexistence, when that occasion was come, which immediately required the application of it. For Jesus had received the baptism of John, which appeared, even to the Baptist, incompatible with the preeminence of the Messias; and he had made no display of that extraordinary might, which John had prophetically attributed to him. These circumstances would rather tend to weaken the effect of the previous declaration of the Baptist, that he, who came after him, was unspeakably his superior in power and dignity. The attribute therefore of preexistence seems to have been dictated by the Spirit, and to have been ascribed to the Messias by the Baptist, in order to aggrandize his character, upon a new and stronger ground, at that time, and under those particular circumstances, when it was most immediately required. This attribute appears to have been grounded upon that interpretation of the title, Son of God, which the Holy Spirit, the continual guide and instructor of the Baptist, in all necessary cases, had suggested to him upon this occasion; and he seems to have been led by the same divine influence, to ground upon that title, other characters of the Messias, which remain to be considered in their place.

But to proceed — During the temptation of the Messias, the Jewish council, by a deputation of priests and Levites to John, inquired into the divine character, which he assumed. It was the [q] prerogative of that council, to examine and decide upon every claim of this kind; and the answer of the Baptist, to this judicial message, was to constitute that evidence, upon which the council virtually professed to admit or disallow his divine mission. This is implied in the language of the messengers; "who art thou? that we may give an answer to them that sent us." It may therefore be expected, that the answer of the Baptist, upon this occasion, should produce the true criterion of his prophetical character. His reply accordingly assigned it. After therein explaining the nature, and limiting the extent, of his office, he attested, as he had done most probably during the last forty days, that the Messias

---

[q] This is implied in Luke xiii. 33. — See Lightfoot Harmony, 2d part 521.

had really appeared, and would speedily manifest himself openly in his preeminent ministry; "there ⁱ standeth one among you, whom ye know not; he it is, who, coming after me, is preferred before me." By this answer, he virtually gave testimony to the council itself, that the Messias was absolutely come, and, by his actual appearance in Israel, had fulfilled that prophecy of his approach, which, as they knew, John constantly had delivered, during that period, in which he had baptized Jerusalem, and all Judæa, and the region round about Jordan. So that, in fact, he urged the accomplishment of his capital prophecy, as forerunner, in proof of his mission from God; and it was formerly observed, that this criterion was the intended and sufficient evidence of it.

Besides, "ˢ these things were done, in Bethabara, where John was baptizing," and therefore, most probably, in the hearing of some disciples, who had seen Jesus receive baptism, and heard their master almost immediately testify, "this was he;" and consequently were enabled to corroborate, what the Baptist

---

ʳ John i. 26. Wolf. ad l. "Standeth, i. e. ministereth." Comp. Zech. iii. 7. Grot. ad John iii. 29.

ˢ John i. 28.

affirmed in his answer to the Levites. The information then, which the messengers had an opportunity of carrying back from Bethabara to the council, was particular and ample, as it comprehended both these circumstances; first, that John really bore a divine commission, since his prediction, of the immediate approach of the Messias, had been fulfilled; and, lastly, that the Messias, upon receiving his baptism, had been openly attested in a miraculous manner from heaven. Thus, that the visit of the Levites to John, happened after he had baptized Jesus, was a circumstance of considerable advantage in the question, concerning the prophetical character of the Baptist, which had been the cause of their coming; for the first certain and unquestionable evidence of the divine mission of John, arose from the baptism of Jesus, and his answer to the messengers accordingly assigned it. The providence of God had, as it seems, so adjusted events and circumstances to the counsel of his own will, that when the claim of the Baptist, to an inspired character, was examined by that judicial authority, which prescribed to the people in allowing or rejecting it, he had been already enabled to assign the completion of his

prophecy,

prophecy, as forerunner, for a plain credential of his divine commission; which he could not have done, at any period of his ministry, prior to the baptism of Jesus. And since the council did not condemn him for a false prophet, they ought in obedience to the law, and upon their own principles, to have received his testimony, as a true one.

To proceed; On the next day, [t] as it appears, to the visit of the Levites, Jesus returned from the temptation, and presented himself again to John. This first opportunity of executing his office, in the utmost extent, was immediately embraced by the Baptist, and he applied to him this signal and interesting attribute, " Behold, the Lamb of God!" This indication of the Messias is personal, and, as such, John immediately pursues it; " this is he, of whom I said, after me cometh a man, which is preferred before me."

When he thus styled him personally, Lamb of God, he seems to have respected the sacrifice of Christ for sin, as the remainder of the clause implies, " who taketh away the sins of the world."

[t] See John i. 29.

Indeed

Indeed, all the piacular oblations of the law, whether made day by day continually, or only at stated times, had their consummation in him, as their antitype; and that the "paschal Lamb, in particular, was a type of the Messias, appears evident from the Scriptural application of the prophecy, " ʷ a bone of him shall not be broken;" and the passover, in the Jewish sense, denoted redemption. But the Messiah cannot be considered as a just antitype, either to the Lamb of the daily sacrifice, or to that of the passover, unless his death had an expiatory purpose and effect. Accordingly, the Apostles represent him sacrificed for us, as a Lamb without spot, and as our passover. He has obtained the redemption of man, not merely because he was spotless, but also, because he was slain; partly, by his unblemished righteousness, but much more, by his precious blood. So that by the full import of the

---

ᵘ The Baptist alludes, either to the Lamb of the daily sacrifice, (Lightfoot's Harmony, 2d part 529) or to the Paschal Lamb, Bochart Hieroz. part 1st. Lib. ii. C. 50. See Huet. D. E. 729.——Deyling. Obs. Sacr. p. 254. part iii. —Epiphan. Hæres. 8. Frischmuth. Diff. de Agno Paschali.— 1 Pet. i. 19. Rom. iii. 25. v. 9. Heb. ix. 14. x. 19. Apoc. v. 9, 7. 14.

ʷ Psalm xxxiv. 20. John xix. 36.

attribute

attribute, Lamb of God, the Baptist, in fact, opposed Jesus to all the Levitical offerings, and pointed him out as the great sacrifice, which God had ordained, and would accept, for universal expiation of sin. It may be further observed from this attribute, that the character of the Messiah seems now to have been revealed to John, more extensively, than before. For, the Baptist had prophetically represented him, as the object of faith, and given testimony that the Father from heaven had declared himself well-pleased in him, as his beloved Son; but he had not hitherto assigned, the principal ground of that faith, or the reason of that good pleasure. But John, at once, enlarged his former prediction, and carried it to the utmost extent; and also, illustrated fully the force and import of the Voice from heaven, by now ascribing both remission of sins, and the good pleasure of the Father, to the sacrifice of the Messiah, as Lamb of God. And, as the disciples of Christ understood not this character of the Messias, till he had opened their understandings, after his resurrection, and given them a clearer notion of that attribute; so neither, it may be presumed, could John have seen and assigned the real ground of human justification,

tion, and of the Father's good-pleasure, in the Messias, without a divine revelation, of more extent and precision, than could be traced in his doctrine, before the baptism of Jesus. For the attribute, Lamb of God, implies the whole of that which an Apostle, after the descent of the Holy Spirit on the disciples, thus comprehensively described[x]; " God hath predestinated us unto the adoption of children by Jesus Christ, according to the good pleasure of his will, to the praise of the glory of his grace, wherein he hath made us accepted in the Beloved, in whom we have redemption through his blood, the forgiveness of sins." As the Messias came principally to fulfil this character of redeemer by his death, it was impossible to point him out to the people, by a more striking and endearing attribute. And, upon this occasion, the Gospel-writer accumulates some preceding testimonies of the Baptist, and represents him as applying them all personally to Jesus. "[y] Behold the Lamb of God, which taketh away the sins of the world! This is he, of whom I said, after me cometh a man, which is preferred before me: for he was before me — and I knew

[x] Eph. i. 5.   [y] John i. 29.

him

him not; but that he should be made manifest unto Israel, therefore am I come baptizing with water — (and John bare record, saying, I saw the Spirit, descending from heaven, like a dove, and it abode upon him) and I knew him not; but he that sent me to baptize with water, the same said unto me, upon whom thou shalt see the Spirit descending and remaining on him; the same is he which baptizeth with the Holy Ghost; and I saw, and bare record that this is the Son of God." As the great personal attribute, Son of God, in the close of this extract, will be considered in the next discourse; some observations, upon a part only of this passage, remain to be offered at present.

The Baptist asserts; " I knew him not, but that he should be made manifest unto Israel, therefore am I come, baptizing with water." Upon applying here what was [z] formerly observed on the assertion, " I knew not," this whole clause may possibly be allowed to import, that the purpose of the baptismal ministry, namely, to manifest the Messias to Israel, was revealed to John, when he received the commission to baptize; but that the individual person of the Messias, and the

[z] See the close of last discourse.

particular incident, wherein he would become known to John, as such, were neither of them revealed to him, at his original call, or at any time, that preceded the coming of Jesus to Jordan. It was then, that he ceased to be strictly the forerunner, and became properly a witness; and it was then, that he knew him by another revelation. The whole verse is set down by the Gospel-writer, as the continued language of the Baptist. This circumstance, as it appears, requires to be carefully noted; for the case seems otherwise with the verse ensuing. In that, the Evangelist breaks off the words of the Baptist, to assign that eminent instance, wherein the baptism of water had, in fact, brought on the manifestation of the Messias to Israel. He speaks in his own person, though he applies the express testimony of the Baptist to the great incident.—
" And John bare record, saying, I saw the Spirit descending from heaven, like a dove, and it abode upon him." The verse seems elliptical, and may be thus filled up, by recurring to the words that preceded; and John bare record, saying, the baptism of water did really manifest the Messias to Israel, forasmuch as I saw the Spirit descending from heaven, and it abode upon him, ὅτι τεθέαμαι

τεθέαμαι τὸ πνεῦμα. This [y] parenthesis of the Gospel-writer specifies only from what circumstance John manifested the Messias to Israel, not that from which the Baptist knew him. On account of that period, which he had thus interposed, and to restore the connection between the verse, immediately following the parenthesis, and that which preceded it, and to alleviate the interruption, which the Evangelist had occasioned by thus interposing a sentence, he has repeated the disclaiming clause, "I knew him not," and with it again introduced the express words of the Baptist. If therefore the first and last of the three verses be thrown together, and the repetition still preserved, their import may be thus represented; I knew him not, but was expressly sent to manifest him unto Israel by the baptism of water. — I knew

---

[y] Another instance of a parenthesis, somewhat similar to this, occurs in ver. 14. of this chapter,—Ὁ λόγος σὰρξ ἐγένετο, ϗ ἐσκήνωσεν ἐν ἡμῖν (ϗ ἐθεασάμεθα τὴν δόξαν αὐτοῦ, δόξαν ὡς μονογενοῦς παρὰ πατρὸς) πλήρης χάριτος ϗ ἀληθείας. There will be no necessity, with some critics, for understanding πλήρης, as put for the accusative, πλήρη, if the parenthesis here be taken as a whole by itself, in which the Evangelist gave an instance, of the visible glory of the Logos, in his tabernacle of the flesh, namely, in the Transfiguration, to which Peter refers in his second Epistle, i. 17, 18.

him not, but was informed that he it was, on whom I should see the Spirit descend and abide, who should baptize with the Holy Ghost. The Baptist mentions two points, that were made known to him at his original call, and also indicates another, that was left, at that time, unrevealed; and he appears not to have given any intimation, that he should not, or that he did not, know the Messias, till the visible descent of the Spirit upon him.

The inconsistency, which has been supposed to subsist between the assertion, "I knew him not," and his words to Jesus, at Jordan, "I have need to be baptized of thee," seems entirely to have arisen, from extending the meaning of the clause, I knew him not, beyond that point of time, when Jesus presented himself to be baptized. At that instant, as it was before observed, he became known to John, and continued so, while he performed his baptismal office, and when the Spirit descended; and the Baptist seems not, either in this passage or any other, to have given just ground for supposing, that he baptized Jesus upon any other footing, than as the Messias, confessedly
known;

known; and has only said, that him, whom he was sent to manifest, and on whom he should see the Spirit descend, he knew not. This seems the whole import of the verses; and they relate rather to the means of manifesting the Messias to Israel, than of revealing him to John; which points appear entirely distinct, and materially different. For this sensible sign was the evidence, intended to be given by John, of the divine character of Jesus. This use of it was at first explained to him, and to this he was directed. And although the sign did not notify the Messias to him, yet it was of great weight in the prosecution of his office. It made him a witness, in that same instance, wherein he had been only a prophet before. His former prediction might still be delivered, but with the advantage of being confirmed and justified by the sign—" he shall baptize you with the Holy Ghost," for I saw it descend and abide upon him. And when the Baptist attested the descent of the Spirit upon Jesus, he appealed, in fact, to a signal and publick miracle, in behalf of his own inspired character. As he did no miracle, he could not have asserted, " this is the Son of God," upon any stronger ground, than divine revelation to himself,

himself, if the sensible sign, of the descent of the Spirit upon Jesus, could not have been urged by him, as a divine attestation to his own veracity. So that the sign was of great importance, even to the Baptist, although it was not wanted to notify the Messias to him.

This passage then, if the illustration of it, here offered, may be admitted, will tend, together with the general substance of this discourse, to support the following conclusions — that, authority to act, as the forerunner and witness to the Messias, was given to John, at his call, but that a considerable part of his qualifications, for the discharge of those offices, was imparted to him, during his ministry; and that, as he could not have undertaken such a baptism of water, and have known the divine purpose, intended by it, except by the word of the Lord originally; so neither could he thus have conducted it with success, through situations, which he did not foresee, without continual inspiration from God.

SERMON V.

JOHN i. 7.

The same came for a witness, to bear witness of the light, that all men through him might believe.

THE baptismal doctrines and prophecies of John, as the forerunner, have been already discussed; but his testimonies, as the witness of the Messias, having been, as yet, illustrated only in part, I proceed, at present, to speak of those, which were delivered by the Baptist, after Christ had actually collected disciples, and assumed a prophetical character.

For this purpose, the great attribute of Christ, as Son of God, may properly be considered; and as the sense, in which John under-

understood that title, may perhaps be determined by those testimonies, that will occur in the present discourse, the illustration of that attribute has been reserved to this place.

" I saw and [a] bare record, that this is the Son of God." The words may possibly imply, that John had commonly ascribed this title to Jesus, before he returned from the temptation, and had again presented himself to the Baptist. But however that may be, the attribute is here applied personally to Jesus; and the words of the Baptist bear an evident reference, both to the descent of the Spirit upon Jesus, which he saw, and to the voice of the Father, which he heard. The descent of the Spirit, was a sign, to him and to the people, that Jesus should baptize with the Holy Ghost; and the Voice from heaven, was a new revelation, that he was the beloved Son of God. The Baptist, as the witness to the Messiah, was thereby enabled to assign the ground of those attributes, which, as forerunner, he had prophetically ascribed to him; and the words of the Father, " thou art my beloved Son," as

[a] " μεμαρτύρηκα, have borne record."

SERMON V.

they were understood by John, immediately led to the attribute, "he was before me," which the Baptist had not ascribed to the Messias, till after the Voice from heaven. What John asserted in that attribute, was equally true of the Messiah's ministry, as a prophet, and of his existence, as a man. He came after the Baptist in both respects; and of course, the attribute, "he was before me," had no relation to either of these senses; for, upon that footing, John would directly contradict his own previous testimony, as well as the rest of the Gospel-history of Christ. It seems then, that, whatever authority the title, beloved Son of God, gave the Baptist, for representing Jesus, as antecedent to him, it must afford him the same for asserting, that Jesus pre-existed as Son of God; and therefore, that he applied this title personally to him, in that strict sense, wherein Jesus afterwards assumed it.

But other expressions of the Baptist, in the further discharge of his office, as a witness, will contribute to shew, that he applied the attribute, beloved Son of God, as expressive of personal, and not only of official, dignity in Christ.

For,

For, soon after his baptism, Jesus began to call disciples, and at Jerusalem, during the Passover, authoritatively [b] expelled from the temple, those who profaned his Father's house, wrought miracles, and delivered his doctrines openly. His disciples also, acting under his immediate commission, [c] baptized the people in Judæa, unto faith in the Messiah, as John did before, and [d] even at that very time; and Jesus returned not into Galilee, until he "[e] knew how the Pharisees had heard that he made and baptized more disciples, than John." It seems to have been his intention, to bring on a comparison between himself and the Baptist; that occasion might from thence be given to John, before his own ministry expired, of bearing testimony to Jesus in the actual exercise of his prophetical office.

Accordingly, a dispute arose concerning the two baptisms, in which the disciples of John took the lead against the Jews, and complained to their master, that his province was invaded, and the credit and success of his own ministry surpassed. "[f] Rabbi, he that

---

[b] John. ii. 15.   [c] John iii. 22. compared with iv. 2.
[d] John iii. 23.   [e] John iv. 1.   [f] John iii. 26.

was with thee beyond Jordan, to whom thou barest witness, behold, the same baptizeth, and all men come unto him." This drew from the Baptist an answer, that, in some particulars, strongly implies, in what an exalted sense he applied the title, Son of God.

He began with assuring his disciples, that the success of Jesus, and his own, were both given from above, in a just proportion to the disparity of their offices; since he was the forerunner only, but Jesus was the [g] Bridegroom and [h] Lord of the Church, that spiritual bride, which was destined for him alone. — if she was disposed to meet him with affection and duty; if she was received and welcomed with his favour, it was all, that his own mission from God had given him [i] to accomplish; it was all, that it left him to desire — " this my joy therefore is fulfilled" — he must increase, but I must decrease."

After this, he enlarges on the dignity of Christ, considering him, as he goes on, in

---

[g] Isaiah liv. 5, 6. lxii. 5. Jerem. iii. 14. Matth. xxii. 2. Ephes. v. 27. Rev. xxi. 9.
[h] Psalm xlv. 11.   [i] 2 Corinth. xi. 2.

the light of a publick teacher, at that time actually discharging his office.

"He that cometh from above, is [k] above all."—— He taught, what the Apostles afterwards more fully set forth, that the Messiah was not taken from among men, but came down [l] from heaven —— [m] that he had by inheritance obtained a more excellent name than angels, and, both by his mission and original, was above all, whether [n] prophets of the earth, or [o] ministering spirits of heaven.

"What he hath seen and heard that he testifieth" —— Prophets, who came not immediately from heaven, and were not, like Him, "above all," could make no fuller discoveries to men of divine things, than their imperfect faculties were able to receive. But the testimony of the Son of God is founded upon his own unlimited and intuitive knowledge.

"And no man receiveth his testimony." —— This seems a direct prophecy of the Messiah's rejection by the Jews; but without contradicting a preceding clause, "he must

---

[k] Rom. ix. 5. Compare 1 Corinth. xv. 47.
[l] John iii. 31. [m] Hebr. i. 4. [n] Heb. i. 1, 2.
[o] Heb. i. 14.

increase."

increase." Their relation is different; for the success of the Messiah's ministry is one thing, but his rejection by the body of the Israelitish nation, is another; and both are predicted by the Baptist.

"He that hath received his testimony hath ᵖ set to his seal, that God is true." Hitherto the law and the prophets had prophesied; but now the age of accomplishment was come. Christ is the end of the law, and ᵠ the vision and the prophecy are sealed up, as "ʳ all the promises of God in him are Yea and Amen." The testimony of Jesus accordingly yields the great and ultimate demonstration of the truth of God, with respect, both to his promises by the prophets, and to the witness, which he had borne to Jesus, by his voice from heaven.

"ˢ For he, whom God hath sent, speaketh the words of God."— All divine messengers may be said to have spoken the "words of God;" but "the words of God" are attributed to Jesus, not only in consequence of his divine mission, in which respect he re-

ᵖ See Wolf. Eph. i. 13. ᵠ Dan. ix. 24.
ʳ 2 Cor. i. 20. ˢ See 1 John v. 10, 11.

sembles the earthly prophets; but also, in consequence of his divine original, as the beloved Son of God, which title belongs properly and exclusively to him. The divinity of that doctrine, which Jesus then actually delivered, was necessarily implied by the subsequent clause, — "for God giveth not the Spirit by measure unto him."—From instances, which have occurred, the influence of the Spirit upon John, appeared to be limited; and, all other prophets received it, like him, occasionally, and by measure. But the prerogative of Jesus was transcendent. As ª it pleased the Father, that, "in him all fullness, ᵇ and all the treasures of wisdom and knowledge, should dwell," the Spirit had no attribute, which was not continual and entire in him.

"The Father loveth the Son, and hath given all things into his hand." Here the Baptist alludes to the voice of the Father from heaven; and assigns the proper foundation of the transcendent prerogatives of Jesus, by referring to this title, "thou art my beloved Son." Agreeably to the import of this

_ª Coloss. i. 19. ii. 3.   _ᵇ John xvi. 15.

testimony,

teftimony, Jefus is reprefented elfewhere, in the New Teftament, as the Lord and "heir of all things, even of thofe which the Father himfelf claimeth — fupreme, not only as a Prophet, but alfo, as the King, and Judge of all.

"He that believeth on the Son, hath everlafting life." The juft fhall live by faith in him, for their ʷ life is in the Son — he will confer it upon us, or refufe it, hereafter, as we believe or deny him here. —

This fignal teftimony to Jefus was not delivered long before the imprifonment of the Baptift, in which his miniftry expired. He repeats and enlarges fome particulars, which he had mentioned before; but difplays the whole character of the Meffiah, in much more exprefs and magnificent terms, than he had hitherto employed. The tranfcendent excellence of his official qualifications; juftification ˣ by faith in him; and eternal life, at his difpofal, as the reward of that faith; are all of them evangelical doctrines, confonant

---

ᵘ Matth. xxi. 38. Rom. iv. 13. Heb. i. 2.
ʷ 1 John v. 11
ˣ Not by the works of the law, which was the principle of the Jews.

indeed

indeed to the genuine import of ancient Scripture, but entirely unknown in Israel; and therefore in delivering them, the Baptist acted as a prophet, and in applying them with others, to Jesus, at that time exercising his ministerial office, he acted as a witness.

Some of the principal characters, here ascribed to the Messias; namely, that he came down from heaven, and testified what he had seen and heard, and was above all; appear immediately grounded upon that declaration of the Father from heaven, "thou art my beloved Son." And these, if taken together with another, already mentioned by the Baptist, "he was before me," seem to render it a just conclusion, that the title, Son of God, was applied by John, as the attribute, not simply of the Messiah's office, but also, of his person; and the amount of these testimonies is nearly equivalent to the confession of saint Peter, after long acquaintance with the doctrines and miracles of Jesus, "[y] thou art Christ, the Son of the living God." It seems to have been the divine intention, that the eye of faith should be led on from a view of the glorified humanity of Jesus, to that of his divinity; and, the language of

[y] Matth. xvi. 16.

the

the Baptist was strictly accommodated to that design, by representing the title, beloved Son of God, as implying not only the extraordinary gifts, and transcendent eminence of Jesus, as a prophet, but also his pre-existence in heaven, and near relation to the Father.

Thus, the Baptist acted, for some space of time, as the forerunner, and for a much longer, as the witness of the Messiah. He knew him not, while he continued merely his forerunner, and prepared the Jews, by baptism, and by the correction of their principles and manners, to expect and receive him with faith. Upon the public appearance of Jesus, John first knew him by immediate revelation; and, at his requisition, and against the previous dictate of his own mind, baptized him, to his office. It was then he became a witness; and immediately notified his actual appearance, and afterwards testified, that he saw the Holy Spirit then descend and abide upon him, and heard the Father, from heaven, pronounce him, his beloved Son. Erelong he publickly pointed him out in person, as the Son of God, attested by that sign, and proclaimed by that voice, from heaven; and upon the
expressions

expressions then used by the Father, and interpreted by the Spirit to the Baptist, he grounded, and ascribed personally to Jesus, the character of universal redeemer; and asserted his pre-existence in heaven, and descent from thence, his personal and unlimited knowledge of divine things, and the immeasureable fullness of his spiritual gifts and powers, his universal superiority and dominion, and the nearness of his relation to God, as his beloved Son. And further, when Jesus actually entered upon his office, and authorized his disciples to baptize, and, in the number of his followers, surpassed the success of John; he knew and felt that the purpose of his own mission was answered; and in terms of great energy, and highly expressive of his eminent humility and pious resignation, he even prophesied that the conclusion of his office was near; "he that hath the bride, is the bridegroom; but the friend of the bridegroom, which [y] standeth and heareth him, rejoiceth greatly because of the Bridegroom's voice: this my joy therefore is fulfilled; he must increase, but I must decrease.

[y] i. e. ministereth. Comp. Zech. iii. 7. Grot. ad l.

SERMON V.

That event soon followed, which verified the prediction of the Baptist. For his ministry, the success of which declined upon the growing manifestation of Jesus in Judæa, was brought very near its close by his imprisonment. Yet that " burning and shining light," in which the people had been willing to rejoice for a season, though rendered faint and dim, did not immediately expire. For it may perhaps appear, upon examination, that, even in the prison, he endeavoured to promote the reception of the Messias, and still acted the part of a witness to Jesus, then fully exercising his great office.

In order to illustrate this point, it must be previously observed, that, upon the imprisonment of the Baptist, Jesus went from Judæa into Galilee, and there [2] preached, " repent ye and believe the Gospel;" he called the Twelve, and attested his divine mission by signs and wonders, accompanied with every circumstance, that might tend to render them illustrious and convincing. Accordingly, " [a] there came a fear on all, and they glorified God, saying, that a great prophet is risen up among us, and that

[2] Mark i. 15.   [a] Luke vii. 16.

God

God hath visited his people. And this rumour of him went forth throughout all Judæa, and throughout all the region round about." Jesus then notoriously verified that signal prophecy of the Baptist, " he, that cometh after me, is mightier than I"—and as that natural and just remark, " [a] all things, that John spake of this man, were true," was delivered before the passion of Christ, it evidently related to his mighty works and doctrines, as confessedly predicted by the Baptist. The powerful effect of the works of Christ, upon the minds of the people, in general, seems not to have exceeded their impression, upon the disciples of the Baptist. In the prison, they acquainted him with the doctrines of Jesus, with his call of the Apostles, and his miracles. That jealousy for the honour of their master, which had already led them to make a similar representation to him of the success of Jesus, was probably one of their present inducements to shew him of all these things. Upon receiving this intelligence, the Baptist " called unto him two of these disciples," and [b] sent them unto Jesus, saying,

---

[a] John x. 41.
[b] Of this message see Episcop. Instit. Theol. Lib. iii. Cap. 25. Jortin. Disc. on Christianity, ch. 5. Macknight on Harmony, §. 42. Lightfoot on Matth. xi. 3.   " Art

" Art thou he, that should come, or do we look for another?" The considerations, that immediately follow, may perhaps have some tendency to explain and justify this conduct of the Baptist.

This message is placed, by St. Luke, immediately after his account of the raising of the widow's son from the dead; and the mighty works of Jesus probably had induced the disciples of John to admit, like Nicodemus, and ^c other Jews, that he was " a teacher come from God." For this appears implied in the very terms and tenor of the question; as it seems strictly calculated to bring on a determination, not whether Jesus bore any, but what, divine character; " art thou he, that should come, or do we look for another? art thou the Messias himself, or only comest thou before him?"

To explain and confirm this construction, it may be observed, that the Jews universally believed that Elias must first come. In consequence of this received opinion, the messengers of the council had enquired of the

---

^c Others of the Jews, who looked not on him, as the Messiah, yet, it is said believed on him on account of his miracles. John vii. 31. Stillingf. O. S. B. ii. Ch. 9. 259.

Baptist himself, "art thou Elias?" and as he answered, "I am not," the publick expectation of Elias, to precede the Messiah, would remain no less prevalent than before, although John was taken for a prophet; and there are evident traces of it, in the Gospel-history, at a later period.

It may be added, that Elias was highly celebrated in Israel, on account of his miraculous power. The son of Sirach delivers the Jewish opinion in this case: "[d] O Elias, how wast thou honoured in thy wondrous deeds, and who may glory like unto thee; who didst raise up a dead man from death, and his soul from the place of the dead, by the word of the most High! The miracles of Jesus, and especially his raising two persons from the dead, might therefore, it may be conceived, rather incline the Jews to take him for Elias. ——

Lastly, it may be remarked, that the Messiah was expected to manifest himself in outward splendor and majesty. The humble state of Jesus would therefore naturally dispose the people to believe, that the character of Messiah could not belong to him.

[d] Ecclus. xlviii. 4.

From

SERMON V.

From these considerations, taken in aid of each other, namely, that, [d] according to the Jewish opinions, Elias was then to come; and that, as Jesus wrought miracles, he was the more likely to be really Elias; but, as he did not appear in outward pomp and greatness, could not, as they apprehended, be the Messiah; it may perhaps seem credible, that these disciples of John, [e] like many of their countrymen, mistook Jesus for Elias; and that it was the real wish and design of the Baptist, to correct this particular error, by so framing the question, as necessarily to bring on a decision of the point in doubt; " art thou he, that should come, or do we look for another," art thou the Messias, or only comest thou before him?

The Baptist evidently knew the real character of Jesus; and any supposition that he made this enquiry, for his own sake, seems irreconcilable with the whole of his former conduct, as the witness of the Messiah, and particularly with that full and eminent testimony, to which he had been led by the for-

---

[d] Trypho objects to Justin, that Elias must first come, to anoint the Messiah. Whitb. on Matth. xvii. 10.
[e] Matth. xvi. 14. Luke ix. 8.

mer report of his followers, that Jesus baptized, and all men came unto him. It may then be reasonably supposed, that the Baptist acted from a leading regard to his disciples, and not to himself.

In order to account for his sending them to Jesus, it may be observed, that he had often attested his divine character at large to all his disciples; 'some of whom had made the right use of his testimony, and consequently followed Jesus. But these disciples of John had acted otherwise, and by obstinately adhering to their master, disappointed his endeavours, and frustrated the great end of his mission. In these circumstances, the Baptist could have little reliance on the effect of his own exhortations, and might rather choose to refer his disciples to Jesus, than, in his own person, to repeat testimonies, which, however express and frequent, had made no proper impression upon them. —

Besides; if he had renewed his own testimonies to the real character of Jesus, even with success, the same effect would but then have followed, which the message itself brought

f John i. 36, 37.

on. In either cafe, the difciples would have repaired to Jefus, and would thereby have fallen under the immediate influence of his doctrines and miracles; and they had unqueftionably the fame power to convince the followers of John, whatever it was, whether the teftimony, or the meffage, of their mafter, that gave them occafion to hear thofe doctrines, and to fee thofe miracles. But the teftimony of the Baptift, if it had been repeated, might not have rendered them more ready, at this time, than before, to follow Jefus, and to inform themfelves of the nature and evidence of his divine character. But this effect, which was all that could be hoped, and which might probably not have followed, from the mere teftimony of John, he now abfolutely enfured by fending the difciples with fuch a queftion to Jefus.

To thefe confiderations it may be added further, that the miracles of Jefus had afforded the ground of that attribute, " he, that cometh after me, is mightier than I," and were greater witnefs to Jefus, than that of John. The Baptift therefore, by fending the difciples to Chrift, really fhewed them the accomplifhment of his own prophetical testimony, and placed them under the immediate impression of that witness to the divine character of Jesus, which far surpassed any testimony, that he either was then, or had been at any time, enabled to give.

If then the message of the Baptist may be placed in this light, he will probably seem to have proceeded in the surest, and therefore in the kindest, way, to promote the spiritual advantage of his followers; and his conduct, in this respect, may appear most suitable, to one great purpose of his mission, that of pointing out the person of the Messiah, and leading the people to him; as well as to the view, under which he appeared to think and act, at all times after the publick appearance of the Messiah, of discouraging an exclusive adherence, and even any leading regard, to himself. ———

Jesus referred the disciples to the present evidence of his miracles and doctrines, as sufficient to determine their question. The things, which they then saw, plainly shewed that he bore some divine character; and, as it belonged not to the forerunner, but to the Messias himself, to preach the Gospel, the things, which they heard, ascertained that
he

he was not Elias, and that they were not to look for another; and his intimations, that the poor had the Gospel preached to them, and that all were blessed, who should not be offended in him, were both of them obviously suited to prevent his lowly condition, from rendering them averse to believe that he really was, " he that should come."

They were, at the same time, directed to go and shew John again the things, which they had heard and seen. As he had dictated their question, and was held by them in the highest reverence, an application of that evidence, which they had heard and seen, was likely to come the nearer to their hearts, when he should explain, and enforce it upon them. And, as Jesus commonly declined to bear testimony to himself, and to assert directly that he was the Messias, it may seem probable, that in this instance, as in all others, he would have left the operation of his doctrines and miracles, upon the minds of John's disciples, to themselves, if it had not been the absolute office of their master to notify the Messiah to the people.

If the turn now given to this meſſage may be admitted, the Baptiſt will appear to have been, even during his impriſonment, a witneſs to Jeſus, and to have maintained to the laſt, that conviction, under which he had acted formerly, that Jeſus was the Meſſiah. Hence alſo, that illuſtrious teſtimony to the character of the Baptiſt, which Jeſus delivered, immediately as the meſſengers of John departed, will ſeem to have an eaſy and natural introduction. He was not " a reed, ſhaken with the wind;" but immovable in principle, and ſteady in teſtimony. He appeared a prophet, in unfolding the genuine ſenſe of former prophecies, and enforcing them with circumſtances, unknown and original; in opening and characterizing the Goſpel-kingdom of the Meſſiah; in proclaiming his immediate approach, and predicting many of his attributes, — and even more than a prophet, in baptizing the Meſſiah to his office, in atteſting his actual preſence, in pointing him out in perſon, as the redeemer and ſanctifier of the world, and the Son of God.

The proper application of thefe prophecies and this teftimony of John, has been made by the mighty one, whofe forerunner and witnefs he was; "[g] if ye will receive it, this is Elias that was for to come — he that hath ears to hear, let him hear."

[g] Matth. xi. 14.

SERMON VI.

JOHN xiii. 19.

Now I tell you before it come, that when it is come to pass, ye may believe that I am he.

IT has been shewn already, that the Baptist, as the forerunner of the Messias, had predicted his coming, and had indicated some of his attributes; and, as a witness, had pointed out Jesus of Nazareth personally, as the mighty one, that should come, the Spirit of God having visibly descended from heaven and abode upon him, and the voice of the Father having, at the same time, declared him his beloved Son.

In order to shew, both the completion of the prophecy, delivered by the Baptist, as forerunner, and the truth of his testimony, as

the

the witness of the Messiah; I proceed, in the subsequent part of these discourses, to assign some of the many signal evidences, which the Holy Spirit gave of his continually dwelling in Jesus, during his publick ministry, by producing and illustrating several of his prophecies, which either immediately related to characters, that John had attributed to him, or were parallel to prophecies, delivered by the Baptist.

The first attribute, which John prophetically ascribed to the Messiah, was contained in the following words; " he, that cometh after me, is mightier than I." As the ancient Scriptures had predicted the miracles of the Messias, and were, ⁜ in that respect, though not in all, rightly understood by the Jews, the attribute of power was confessedly the great characteristic of his ministry. And Jesus appropriated to himself this prophetical character, by openly exerting a mighty power, at his will, by his word, at hand or at a distance, upon animate or inanimate nature, and over the invisible world; against him that had

⁜ See Grot. on John ix. 32.

the

the power of death, and against the spirits of darkness. Jesus fulfilled the prophecy of the Baptist, by this exercise of power; and also verified his testimony, by thus sensibly displaying that glory, which he received at Jordan. For, as Jesus cast out devils by the Spirit of God, and as the Father, that dwelt in him, did the works, his signs and wonders were the witness, both of the Spirit, that descended from heaven, and rested upon him, and [c] of the Father, whose voice declared him his beloved Son.

As the reality, and divinity, of the miracles of Jesus are points, that fall not properly within the plan of these discourses, which treat of his prophecies only; it will not be allowable to offer more than a short observation or two upon them.

As all sensible facts whatsoever are credible upon adequate testimony, it seems that they will not become incredible, merely because they are miraculous. The only question then, that can be reasonably made, respects the sufficiency of the evidence.
Nor will the regularity of the operations of

[c] John xiv. 10.

nature

nature afford an insuperable objection to the credibility of a miracle; for the testimony of eye-witnesses yields greater evidence in behalf of the miracle, than the regularity of nature can bring against it; the one, as positive, ought in reason to overrule the other, as only presumptive. And when the character of the Apostles, and their [d] motives to preach the Gospel, with their number and [e] agreement, and all the circumstances that can be, and have been, urged in their favour, are taken together into consideration; that their testimony should yet, after all, be false, seems infinitely more [f] wonderful, and proportionably less credible, than the very miracles, which they attest.

The credibility of the miracles of Christ must therefore rest, not upon the nature of the facts, but only upon the evidence, that is brought to ascertain them; and, if the testimony of the Apostles cannot reasonably be rejected, all previous questions will be

---

[d] See Stillingfl. O. S. Book ii. Ch. 9. §. 9. Campbell. Auth. Gosp. Hist. Sect. xiv. pag. 152.

[e] See Lactant. de Justitia, Lib. v. cap. 3.

[f] The remark of Chrysostom may be applied to the Apostles, εἰ σημεῖον (Χριστὸ) χωρὶς ἐπεισεν, πολλῷ μεῖζον τὸ θαῦμα φαίνεται. ap. Stillingfl. O. S. B. ii. Ch. 10. §. 5. Hume's Ess. on Miracles, pag. 182, 183.

excluded,

SERMON VI.

excluded, and the miracles of Christ must be admitted, as real.

When the earliest adversaries, to the Gospel, either pretended that [g] miracles were not characteristical evidences of the Messiah; or imputed the mighty works of Christ to magical or diabolical power in him, or attempted to [h] traduce and depreciate them; they seem to have felt the incontestable force of the Apostolical testimony, and virtually to have given up all objection to the reality of the miracles of Jesus. And if enemies to Christianity, so able and determined, as Maimonides,

---

[g] Maimonider, de Reg. cap. xi, says, " do not imagine that the king Messiah shall have any need to alter the course of nature, or to raise the dead. (Bishop Patrick. Witnesses to the Son of God, pag. 181.) — He asserts also, (de fund. leg. cap. viii. 1.) that the Israelites did not believe Moses from the miracles, which he wrought, — and elsewhere, that Elias and Elisha wrought not their miracles to confirm their prophecies. This seems extorted from him by the irresistible evidence of Christ's miracles; for he says, (ibid. vii. §. 12.) we believe not every one that shews a sign, or doth a miracle, to be a prophet, unless we have known him from the beginning, to be fit for prophecy; that, in his wisdom, and his works, he hath excelled his contemporaries, and hath walked in the ways of prophecy, in holiness and separation from others." His reservation probably was, we know not what, or whence, Christ is, and therefore his miracles are no evidence at all. Nihil non nugacissimi mortalium fingunt, ne cogantur agnoscere, virtute ac digito *quasi* ipsius Dei, Jesum nostrum effecisse miracula sua. Voritius. See Stillingfl. O. S. B. ii. Ch. 6. pag. 202.

[h] Origen. contra Celsum. Lib. i. p. 22, 30.

Celsus,

Celsus, [i] Julian, and [k] others, could not discredit the testimony of the Apostles, and deny that the mighty works of Jesus were real, it seems entirely inconceivable, that exceptions, which appeared unreasonable, in the days of those adversaries, can be made upon any juster ground, in our own, to the testimony of the Apostles, and the reality of the miracles of Christ. And if the reality of the miracles of Christ, cannot justly be disallowed, the divinity of them will necessarily follow from their nature and effect. For, as [l] they tended to overturn the kingdom of the evil spirit, it is [m] plain that they were wrought by the Holy Spirit of God, as the [n] Apostles and Jesus himself asserted.

To return then from this digression and proceed. — There is one view, in which the miracles of Christ may be represented, consistently with the plan of these discourses;

[i] Julian apud Cyrill. l. 6. p. 206.
[k] Hierocles apud Euseb. p. 512.
[l] The substance of those arguments, which are usually urged in defence of Christ's miracles, may be seen in Jortin. Rem. E. H. Vol. ii. p. 7.
[m] See Stillingfl. O. S. B. ii. Ch. 10. p. 352. Origen. contra Celf. Lib. ii. Chrysost. Hom. ad Matth. xii. 25. ὅτι μὲν γὰρ γίνεται, ᾗ ὑμεῖς ἐστέ· ὅτι δὲ θείᾳ δυνάμει γίνεται, ᾗ πράγματα ἐστί.
[n] Acts ii. 11.

namely,

namely, as far as they admitted a prophetical application, or gave him immediate occasion to deliver prophecies.

1. A miraculous draught of fishes struck the disciple Peter with astonishment and dismay. Upon seeing what the power of Christ could accomplish, he dreaded what it might inflict; "° depart from me, for I am a sinful man, O Lord." Christ immediately dispelled his terror, by a prophetical application of the miracle to him; "fear not, from henceforth thou shalt catch men." He extended the same promise to other disciples on a similar occasion; "I will make you fishers of men." His power, that gave success to their present toil, would co-operate with them, as effectually, when they should spread the ᵖ net of the Gospel, and gather of every kind.

2. He said unto the man, sick of the palsy, "ᑫ thy sins be forgiven thee;" and proceeds to justify himself for assuming the divine prerogative of forgiving sin. "That ye may know and believe, that the Son of man

° Luke v. 8.   ᵖ Matth. xiii. 47.
ᑫ Matth. ix. 2.

hath

hath power on earth to forgive sins, then saith he to the sick of the palsy, arise, take up thy bed, and go unto thine house." He seems to represent that miraculous cure, as the sign of a much greater, which he would afterwards accomplish; and by thus removing the pains of sickness, prophetically implies, that he would take away ʳ the punishment of sin.   So also, upon giving sight to the eye, he alluded prophetically to his future dispersion of that spiritual darkness, which had hitherto hung over the mind. " I am the light of the world; ˢ I am come into this world, that they, which see not, might see." And from these instances, it seems not improbable, that upon healing other bodily infirmities, he sometimes represented himself, in a prophetical light, as the restorer of ᵗ health to the souls of men, which are often spiritually deaf, and dumb, and lame, and blind.

3. From the miracle of the loaves, he takes occasion to draw off the attention of the people, from " ᵘ the meat which perish-

---

ʳ Chrysost. Hom. 30. pag. 344. Ed. Par. Τῆς μὲν τῶν ἁμαρτημάτων ἀφέσεως τεκμήριον τὴν τοῦ σώματος σφίγξιν ποιεῖται.
ˢ John ix. 5. 39.   ᵗ Matth. ix. 12.
ᵘ John vi. 27.

eth, to that which endureth unto everlasting life;" and prophetically points out his flesh, as that "living bread," which he would give for the life of the world. As he had provided temporal sustenance by the loaves and fishes, so he promised eternal life, through his body and blood; and prophetically represented the present exercise of his power, in dispensing the one, as the sign and pledge of his future display of it, in procuring the other.

4. The [w] seventy disciples, at their mission, were not expressly invested with any other miraculous power, but that [x] of healing the sick. It seems that they proceeded further, than barely to the cure of bodily diseases; for they "returned again with joy, saying, Lord, even the devils are subject unto us through thy name."—

From their expression of joy and wonder, Christ took immediate occasion to represent their success in a prophetical light; "I beheld Satan, like lightning, fall from heaven." His view went on from their past to their future efforts against the evil spirit; and he marked their present triumph over

[w] Luke x. 1. [x] v. 19.

him, as the sign and prelude of his final ruin. Accordingly, he delivers an immediate promise to them; "behold I give unto you power to tread on serpents and scorpions, and over [y] all the power of the enemy. Upon his mission of the twelve to the cities of Israel, he had given them the same "[z] authority over all devils, and to cure diseases." At the time of his conferring this power upon them, he had an evident view to their [a] second mission, "go ye into all the world, and preach the Gospel to every creature." And when he gave this command, after his resurrection, it was accompanied with his general promise to believers; "[b] in my name shall they cast out devils, they shall speak with new tongues; they shall take up serpents; and if they drink any deadly thing, it shall not hurt them; they shall lay hands on the sick, and they shall recover." With what justice

---

[y] Προφητεία δοκεῖ τὸ λεγόμενον εἶναι — δῆ᾽ ὧν τοίνυν ὅτι ὁ δαίμονας σκοδάλις μόνον, ἀλλὰ καὶ τὴν πλάνην τῆς οἰκουμένης ἅπασαν ἀπιλάσοι, καὶ τὰς μαγγανείας τοῦ Διαβόλου καταλύσοι, καὶ πάντα αὐτοῦσι ποιήσει τα ἐκείνω, ταῦτα ἔρηκε. Chrysostom. Hom. 42. ad Matth. xii. 25. pag. 447. Ed. Par.

[z] Luke ix. 1.

[a] Grotius ad Matth. x. 16. Mark xvi. 15.

[b] Of the accomplishment of this promise, in its several clauses, see Grotius on Mark xvi. 15. sq.

and truth, had the Baptist ascribed to him the attribute of power? It was his will, it was his ^c name, that ^d would co-operate with the faith of his followers; and nothing could baffle, or even withstand, that power, which he would confer upon them.

Lastly, That majestic declaration, "^e I am the resurrection and the life," placed his intended miracle, of raising Lazarus from the dead, in a light doubly prophetical; first, as the pledge of the general resurrection, " he that believeth in me, though he were dead, yet shall he live,"— and secondly, as the assurance of everlasting life after death, "^f he that liveth, and believeth in me, shall never die." He predicted restoration to life, and the inheritance of

---

^c Matth. xii. 27. Mark ix. 38.
^d Transcribere in alium jus suum, et quod facere solus possis, fragilissimæ rei donare, et participare faciendum, super omnia sitæ est potestatis, continentisque sub se omnium rerum causas, et rationum facultatumque naturas. Arnob. Lib. i. p. 31. — Whitby on John xiv. 12.
^e John xi. 25. sq.
^f He that liveth, i. e. after his resurrection, ——— and believeth in me," — this is the condition; for they who believe not, will be delivered up to the power of the second death.

immortality, to all those, who had faith in him, as author and giver of both, and thus appropriated to himself the prophecy of the Baptist, " he that believeth on the Son, hath everlasting life." ———

In these wonders and signs of Christ, the prophecy of John, " he, that cometh after me, is mightier than I," was fulfilled; and the prophetical applications, that Christ made of his mighty works, ascertain his perfect insight into the whole plan of redemption, and his distinct foreknowledge of every succeeding display of his power, till it should have entirely accomplished the good pleasure of the Father. The miracles themselves, and the prophetical views, in which Jesus frequently represented them, suggest a very interesting question, that occurred to the Jews upon another occasion, " ᵍ whence hath this man this wisdom, and these mighty works?" The answer has been already given in the testimony of the Baptist, " I saw the Spirit descending from heaven, and it abode upon him." This display of spiritual gifts, and spiritual might, alike unlimited in knowledge and operation, manifested forth the divine glory

ᵍ Matth. xiii. 54.

of the Spirit that dwelt in Jesus. In a word, by this accumulation of prophecy and miracle, he appeared at once the wisdom, and power, of God.

But to proceed to another character, attributed to him by the Baptist; " behold the Lamb of God." When his miracles had sufficiently " manifested forth his glory," both as to his office, and original, to persuade the disciples, that he was " [h] Christ the Son of the living God," he began to lay before them, [i] without further reserve, the bitter sufferings, which he would undergo, in the accomplishment of his character, as Lamb of God.

He frequently inculcated the great purpose of his passion; " [k] the Son of man came — to minister, and to give his life a ransom for many;" and more explicitly than ever, at the institution of the Holy Communion; " this is my blood of the New-Testament, which is shed for many, for the remission of sins." And agreeably to the true and full import of these and other similar intimations, he thus professes in his prayer to

[h] Matth. xiv. 33. John vi. 69. xxvi. 31. John v. 36, 37. viii. 18. x. 25, 38. Acts viii. 37. xiv. 11.
[i] Mat. xvi. 21. [k] Matth. xx. 28.

the Father, immediately before his death, " for their fakes, I fanctify myfelf." This feems to be a [k] facrifical expreffion, by which he devotes himfelf as an expiatory offering.

Indeed, that the Meffias would be [l] facrificed for the expiation of univerfal fin, had been evidently foretold by the ancient prophets. Many of the indignities, and [m] perhaps the very manner of his death, were by them particularly marked. But the prophecies of Jefus, that refpected his fufferings, appear neverthelefs original in him, not only from his delivering in particular detail, what the prophets had reprefented in general and indefinite terms; but alfo from his enlarging their prophecies, and predicting various things and circumftances, that would befall him, of which no certain traces occur in the Old Teftament. Thefe predictions afcertain his own prophetical character, agreeably to his

---

[k] See Levitic. xxi. 3. comp. Heb. ii. 11. Whitby ad l.
[l] Ifaiah xxxiii. 10. Dan. ix. 7. 26.
[m] Zechariah xii. 10. xiii. 6. Pfalm xxii. 18 This whole pfalm is admitted by the Jews to relate to the Meffias. Huet. Dem. Ev. prop. 9. pag. 607. H. br. ii. 6. Voffius Har. Ev. Lib. ii. 7. §. 48. obferves that there is no prophecy of Chrift's crucifixion in the Old-Teftament.

inference

SERMON VI. 137

inference in the text, "[n] I tell you before it come; that when it is come to pass, ye may believe that I am he."

Thus, he particularized not only the [o]place, but also the day of his passion; "[p] after two days is the feast of the passover, and the Son of man is betrayed to be crucified." At the time of his delivering this prophetical notice, the Jewish assembly [q] had resolved to offer no violence to him, during the festival-week; and the design of betraying him to the chief-priests had not, as it seems, been formed. These circumstances render the prediction, that he should suffer at the passover, more signal and wonderful.

After having frequently declared that he should be delivered into the hands of men, he pointed out one of the twelve, as the betrayer, by a publick and personal designation; and, with a view, as it seems, to the execution of his project, said unto him at the instant, "what thou doest, do quick-

---

[n] John xiii. 19.
[o] Luke xx. 14, ἴδις πῶς ϲϛϙίτιυσι ϗ̇ τ̇ τόπον, ὕϳυ ἱκπνɩ ϲφάϯιαϗ; ϗ̇ ἐκϐάλοιτις (ἴξω ϯ ἀμπιλῶɩϽ) ἀπίκτσιαν. Chrysost. Hom. 68. pag. 671. Ed. Par.
[p] Mat. xxvi. 2.
[q] v. 5.

ly;"

ly;" and immediately, on his going out, "now," he exclaimed, "is the Son of man glorified." From whence it seems a just inference, that the treacherous compact itself; and the design of his betrayer to fulfil it, in that night; and the actual accomplishment of his scheme, in the course of it; were fully and distinctly foreseen. And, even in the moment of its execution, when Judas, at the head of a multitude, drew near, that affecting question, "betrayest thou the Son of man with a kiss," implied his knowledge of that sign, whereby it had been agreed to single him out from the disciples. ——

His assurance to the eleven, "all ye shall be offended because of me this night," although correspondent to a *former prophecy, which he then cited and applied, was yet accompanied with sufficient evidences of his divine foreknowledge. For here also, as before, he enlarged the prophecy. He predicted the repeated denials of Peter, with a limitation as to time. This was entirely original; and the more closely the prediction is considered, the more wonderful will it

* Zechar. xiii. 7.

appear.

appear. This abjuration, when foretold, was not only contingent, but expressly contrary to the resolute determination of that disciple's mind. Yet three repetitions of it were distinctly marked. The case also involves another strong and very interesting circumstance. When Christ stood [s] before his judges, and actually answered the question of the high-priest, respecting his disciples and his doctrine, the several replies of his follower had not escaped him. He marked the moment, when the prediction was fulfilled in all its parts; and then, "[t] the Lord turned, and looked upon Peter," who instantly, "remembered the word, that Jesus had spoken." ———

" He shall be delivered to the Gentiles," was another original prophecy; and upon the completion of it, the peculiar indignities, which he was to suffer, and his crucifixion, all which he expressly foretold, [u] absolutely depended. He was [w] condemned by the Jews for blasphemy, in calling himself the Son of God; and [x] death by stoning was the

[s] John xviii. 19.   [t] Luke xxii. 61.
[u] See John xviii. 31, 32.   [w] Matth. xxvi. 65, &c.
[x] This they actually confess — Behold the man, that is condemned to be stoned. Sanhedr. in Lightfoot, Hor. Heb. et Tal. on Acts. pag. 634.

punish-

punishment, which their law prescribed. But, ʸ as it was " not lawful for them to put any man to death," they led him away to ᶻ the Roman governor; and fearing that Pilate would not be disposed to put Christ to death, for blasphemy against the God of Israel, they changed their ground of accusation, and represented him, as a mover of sedition, and a ᵃ state criminal; " if thou let this man go, thou art not Cæsar's friend; " whosoever maketh himself a king, speaketh against Cæsar." That charge subjected Christ to the ᵇ Julian law, which was executed in the reign of Tiberius with the utmost rigour. Fear of the tyrant, and of the turbulent multitude, who demanded that crucifixion,

---

ʸ Either, because according to their law, crucifixion could not be inflicted; (See Le Clerc. Hamm. on John xviii. 31.—Grot. on Gal. iii. 13.) which nevertheless, and not stoning, they were resolved that Jesus should undergo. Judæi non alio quam crucis supplicio Christum affici volebant, tamen alio potuissent. Gregor. Nyss. 1 Orat. in Ref. Christi.——Or else, on account of the feast, lest they should be defiled, Augustin. Tractat. 114. in Johan. of the same opinion is Chrysostom. ap. Merilli not. Philol. in Cren. Fascic.

ᶻ Tacit. Ann. xv. 44. 114.

ᵃ Luke xxiii. 2. John vii 12.

ᵇ Senec. lib. iii. de benef. cap. 26. Sueton. in Tiberio. cap. xxviii. 1. Tacitus, Ann. 3. xxxviii 1. — addito majestatis crimine, quod tum omnium accusationum complementum erat. ap. Merilli. not. philol. ad Johan. xix. 12. in Cren. Fascic.

prescribed by the Roman law, might be inflicted on him, prevailed over the favourable disposition of the governor to Jesus, and induced him to give sentence, that it should be, as they required. Thus was he delivered up to the soldiers of Pilate, and treated by them according to the ᶜ customs, and ᵈ law of the Romans. The Jews, who had unjustly condemned him to death by their law, constrained the Gentiles to crucify him as unjustly by their own. ᵉ St. Peter afterwards upbraided them with this aggravation of their guilt; " him, by wicked hands, ye have crucified and slain." —

Thus was he " ᶠ numbered with the transgressors," and, " poured out his soul unto death," in full accomplishment of his own assurances, as a prophet, and of his

---

ᶜ Christ was scourged. Matth. xxvii. 26. Mark xv. 15. as being condemned to crucifixion.—Florus also, first scourged those whom he afterwards crucified. Joseph. ubi supra. Titus did the same. Lib. vi. cap. 12.

ᵈ Paul. Lib. v. sentent. tit. 22. Authores seditionum, et tumultûs, concitato populo, pro qualitate conditionis, aut in crucem tolluntur—aut bestiis subjiciuntur, aut in insulam deportantur. The same punishment was inflicted upon others, for sedition, by Varus, and Florus, successors of Pilate. Joseph. de bell. Iud. Lib. ii. cap. 14. Merill. ubi supra.

ᵉ Acts ii. 23. See Huet. Dem. Evang. 61. Locke on Rom. vi. 8. Gal. ii. 15. Benf. Hist. planting Ch. 81.

ᶠ Isai. liii. 12.

lamb

character, as Lamb of God; and even in the midst of unspeakable agony upon the cross, he saw, as at one glance, the compass and extent of prophecy, and the whole scheme and intention of the Father, concerning his sufferings; and, having first verified the prophecies in one only point, that ᶠ yet remained to be fulfilled, pronounced that all, which was written in Scripture, or purposed by the Father, was accomplished; " it is finished," and bowing his head he " gave up the ghost."

From the substance of these particulars, several important inferences evidently arise.

It thence appears, that, as all things, whether they were written in the ancient prophecies, or not, which should come upon him, under every situation and conjuncture, were known to Christ without limitation, he has given the plainest evidence, that his mission, and his doctrines, were divine; and that, according to his frequent assurances, his death was expiatory, and, as such, had been ᵍ foreordained by the Father, and consented to by himself.

ᶠ John xix. 28.

ᵍ See the promise of the Father, Isaiah liii. 7, 10, 11, 12.
───── and the undertaking of the Son, Psalm iv. 7, 8, 9.─────
see also Zechariah vi. 13.

2. It

2. It appears also, that, the human heart, in all its present and future movements, lay open to him. St. Mark [h] attributes this knowledge of the heart, to " his Spirit;" not to prophetical inspiration merely, (for a prophet is not said to know by his spirit) but to his transcendent participation of the essential Word, τῇ ἀκρᾷ μετόχῃ τῦ Αὐτολόγυ, as the apologist to Celsus speaks; and, in [i] Scripture, " the divine nature of Christ, is called the Spirit, — through which he is said to have offered up himself."

It appears also, lastly,[k] that the divine mind, no less than the human, was by him distinctly known; and that, according to the witness of the Baptist, and his own, he testified what he had heard and seen, with the Father, whose words he spake, whom he knew, as the Father knew him, and in whom he was, as the Father in him, his beloved and only-begotten Son.

These predictions related immediately to his character, as Lamb of God; he also

---

[h] ii. 8, Grot. ad loc. See John xvi. 30. Revel. ii. 23.
[i] Heb. ix. 14. 1 Pet. iii. 18.
[k] 1 John v. 8.

delivered

delivered others, that chiefly respected his great attribute, as Son of God, which the Baptist had likewise ascribed to him.

Of this kind was the prophecy of his rising from the dead, which generally accompanied the prediction of his death. He represented his resurrection, as a sign to that generation, evidently, because it would fully " declare him the Son of God;" and his prophecy of that miracle, was not imparted to the disciples only, but delivered at large, and [l] generally known.

[m] Foregoing prophets had strongly implied, rather than expressly named, the Messiah's resurrection from the dead. The terms, in which Christ predicted it, were not only very direct and particular, but also included circumstances, that either were entirely original, or if, in any degree, alluded to in the Old-Testament, were first brought out into light by him. Such instances, therefore, seem fully to evince the reality of his own prophetical character.

---

[l] Matt. xxvii. 63.
[m] Psalm xvi. 10. xli. 1c. Isaiah liii. 10, 11. Acts iii. 1. 1 Pet. i. 11.

SERMON VI.

He refers to ⁿ the case of the prophet Jonah, as exactly denoting the appointed time of his continuance in the grave; and accordingly, his own resurrection, as the great antitype to the miraculous deliverance of the prophet, was limited by himself to ° the third day.

He named, not only the day of his resurrection, but also, the place of his future appearance; "^p after I am risen, I will go before you into Galilee;" and he seems to have appointed a mountain, in that district, where he would shew himself unto the disciples. This prophetical appointment was probably intended to render his appearance, after death, more publick and unquestionable; for, ^q most probably upon that moun-

---

ⁿ Mat. xii. 39, 40. xvi. 4. ——— Rabbini, Jonæ typum pro resurrectione mortuorum confirmandâ citantes, allegant Oseæ dictum, vi. 2. quod sanè cum typo Jona, qui tres dies et tres noctes integras in cete detentus fuisse legitur, non convenit. Ex quo apparet, etiam loca ista, in quibus dicitur Christum resurrecturum, μετὰ τρεῖς ἡμέρας, sic intelligenda esse, ut μετὰ τρεῖς ἡμέρας idem significet, quod intra tres dies, sive tertio post die. Episcop. Instit. Theol. 463. Cap. 17. §. 4.

° Mat. xvi. 21. xvii. 23. xx. 19. Mark ix. 31. x. 34. Luke ix. 22. xiii. 32.

^p Matth. xxvi. 32. See Kidder, D. Mes. Part 3. p. 94.

^q Matth. xxviii. 16. Those who doubted, were not of the eleven, but of the rest, who came thither to see him. See Lightfoot, 1 Cor. xv. 6.

tain in Galilee, he was seen by five hundred brethren at once.

As these circumstances, which Jesus particularly foretold, had not been indicated by any foregoing prophet, it seems a reasonable conclusion, that he possessed an exact knowledge of all the purposes of God, which respected his resurrection, and his appearance to the disciples, after death, entirely personal, and underived from any divine revelation, that preceded his coming.

So far then Jesus has appeared a real prophet, from the prediction, which he delivered, of his rising again from the dead. But there is another original, and extremely signal, circumstance, from which he must appear infinitely more than a prophet.

He not only expressly foretold his resurrection, but also represented it as an act of his own power; " destroy ' this temple, and in three days I will raise it up." The Evangelist informs us, that " he spake of the temple of his body."

The sacred writers, speak of the divinity of Christ, in a style of accommodation to

' John ii. 19. 21.

the

SERMON VI. 147

the common notions of the Jews. They believed that the divine presence was in ⁸ the tabernacle. Accordingly, by the Evangelists and Apostles, the human nature of Christ, is named the temple and ᵗ tabernacle of his divinity, as the Word, or Son of God; ἐσκήνωσεν ἐν ἡμῖν, "he dwelt among us," says St. John, or, in a more close and endearing sense, he tabernacled in our nature; and, "in him dwelleth all the fulness of the Godhead ᵘ bodily," says St. Paul; and hence he elsewhere calls the humanity, or flesh, of Christ, ʷ καταπέτασμα, the veil.

Hence then may be understood his promise of raising his own body from the grave. As his actual resurrection ascertained his prophetical character, because he had foretold it; so also, the completion of his express promise to rise again, by his own power, as strongly implies, that there was in Christ something besides, and far above, a

---

ˢ Levit. xxvi. 11, 12. Ezek. xxxvii. 26. 2 Cor. vi. 16.

ᵗ Ἴδιον αὐτῷ (σάρκα) ποιησάμενος ναὸν, ᾗ ἐν αὐτῇ, ᾗ σὺν αὐτῇ, γνωριζόμενος, ὡς Θεὸς ᾗ Κύριος. Cyrill. ap. Petav. Dogm. Theol. Lib. vii. Ch. 11. §. 11. —— See Vitring. Obs. Sacr. pag. 145. sqq. The human nature of Christ is styled by Epiphanius, δοχεῖον πληρώματος.

ᵘ Col. ii. 9. τύπον, ὡς ἐν ἰδίῳ σώματι τὸ γὰρ ἡμέτερον ἴδιον ἐποιήσατο σῶμα. Paul. Emes. apud Petav. ibid.

ʷ Heb. x. 20.

K 2   mortal

mortal nature. The Apostle Peter accordingly affirms, " [x] that he was put to death in the flesh, but quickened by the Spirit." The flesh and the Spirit, in relation to Christ, are expressions commonly used by the Apostles, to denote, by the [y] first of them, his humanity, and by the last of them, his divinity. Thus he is said, both to have offered himself, and to have been quickened, by the Spirit. There was in him, that which could be sacrificed and die; and there was in him, that which offered up his mortal nature, as a sacrifice, and afterwards [z] raised it again to life. The one was the flesh, which could be put to death; the other was " the eternal Spirit."

Hence he is a quickening Spirit to the human nature, both in himself and in his brethren. As the Son " had life in himself," he was able, according to his prophecy and his promise, to build again that temple of his body, in which the fulness of the Godhead had dwelt; and as he "quickeneth whom he will," and is truth itself, he will

---

[x] 1 Ep. iii. 18.
[y] Rom. i. 3. John i. 14.
[z] It it no objection, that the Father raised him. See John v. 19.

equally

SERMON VI.

equally fulfil his univerfal prophecy and promife, " I am the refurrection and the life."

When he was rifen from the dead, his difciples were enabled to underftand both his prophecy and promife, relating to it. Then " [a] they believed the Scripture," becaufe the refurrection of their Lord was foretold therein; and they believed " the word, which Jefus had faid," becaufe he had, not only predicted it, but alfo promifed perfonally to fulfil it.

Upon this point it may be fufficient to make the following remark. The teftimonies of the Baptift, that the Father gave not the Spirit to Jefus by meafure, and that he had a nature, infinitely fuperior to that, in which he came after John, feem evidently verified by his refurrection from the dead, confidered as the completion of his promife. For, when his human nature was broken and divided, and when he was not a perfect man, he yet perfonally exerted the divine power of the Spirit, to render his manhood again entire. ——

[a] John ii. 22.

The prophecy of his ascension, when the terms, in which Jesus delivered it, are strictly considered, bears an immediate relation to his character, as Son of God, and verifies the testimony of the Baptist, that he came from heaven.

The ascension of the Messiah to heaven, had been alluded to by the prophets, and particularly by the [b] Psalmist, and Daniel. But Jesus delivered this prophecy, not only in terms that were direct, and not indefinite, which alone would evince the reality of his prophetical character; but also, accompanied it with circumstances, which the prophecies of the Psalmist and Daniel had not mentioned, and to which, of course, they did not lead.

He foretold his ascension, as visible to the disciples; "[c] what and if ye shall see the Son of man ascend up where he was before?" He marked this circumstance, in consequence of his own knowledge, that the Father had purposed, and the Gospel-scheme required, that they should see him ascend; and accordingly, [d] while they beheld, he was taken up, and a cloud received him out of their sight."

[b] Psalm lxviii. 18. Dan. vii. 13 [c] John vi. 62. [d] Acts i. 9.

The concluding words of the prophecy, "where he was before," are directly parallel to the testimony of John, that he came "from above;" and to a similar effect, Jesus speaks elsewhere of his ascension to heaven, as of his return to the Father; "[e] and now, O Father, glorify thou me with thine own self, with the glory, which I had with thee, before the world was." The prophet Daniel, although he had spoken rather more largely than the Psalmist, yet represented the Son of man, as receiving only the glory of his mediatorial kingdom; but Jesus has enlarged the prophecy, and expressly referred to another glory, which he had with the Father, not only before the mediatorial kingdom, but even before the world began. It is this capital circumstance, which no prophecy, of the Messiah's ascension to heaven, had mentioned, except his own, that affords the strongest evidence to his character, as a real prophet, and justifies the attributes, ascribed to him by the Baptist, "he was before me," "he that cometh from above," "this is the Son of God."

From the substance of this discourse, one general inference seems to arise; that the

[e] John xvii. 5.

glory of the Godhead in Jesus, shone forth through the vail of his flesh, in miracles of power, combined with such miracles of knowledge, that the confession of his disciples cannot but appear as just, as it was obvious, — "*f* now are we sure, that thou knowest all things, — by this we believe, that thou camest forth from God."

f John xvi. 30.

SERMON VII.

JOHN xiii. 19.

Now I tell you before it come, that when it is come to pass, ye may believe that I am he.

THE prophecies of Jesus, which were considered in the last discourse, were grounded upon characters, prophetically ascribed to him by the Baptist. I proceed, at present, to consider other prophecies of Jesus, which not only had an immediate reference to the character, Son of God, attributed to him by John, but also were parallel to prophecies, that John had previously delivered.

The prediction, of the restoration of the Holy Spirit to the people of God, respected the character of Jesus, not only as a prophet, but also, as Son of God, since it was delivered in the terms both of a prophecy, and a promise.

He uses the following, among other expressions. "[a] I will pray the Father, and he shall give you another Comforter," "even the Spirit of truth," "which is the Holy Ghost;" and he gave the disciples an assurance, something more than prophetical, that the mission of the Spirit, absolutely depended upon his own ascension to the Father; "[a] if I go not away, the Comforter will not come unto you."

He not only predicted the advent, but also promised the mission, of the Holy Ghost. "[b] Behold, I send the promise of my Father upon you;" "[c] I will send him unto you," "from the Father;" and he seems to call the advent of the Spirit, his own coming, and his seeing the disciples again [d]. He also gave a prophetical delineation of the offices of the Holy Spirit, — "he shall teach you all things, and bring all things to your remembrance, whatsoever I have said unto you," "he shall testify of me," "and he will

---

[z] John xiv. 16, &c.   [a] John xvi. 7.   [b] Luke xxiv. 49.
[c] John xvi. 7.   [d] John xiv. 18, 19, 28. comp.
Gal. iv. 6. Phil. i 19.

shew

SERMON VII.

shew you things to come; [e] he shall glorify me, for he shall receive of mine, and shall shew it unto you." And he assigns the true ground, both of his promise to send the Spirit unto them, and of this prophetical account of his offices; "[f] all things, that the Father hath, are mine; therefore said I, that he shall take of mine, and shall shew it unto you." In these passages, the Holy Spirit is described as another divine agent, in the work of redemption; as a witness, to attest that Christ was gone to the Father, and, as an advocate, to glorify him, by preparing the Apostles, in all respects, to fulfil the commission, which he had given them, to preach the Gospel, and by abiding with his flock for ever.

The parting address of Jesus to the disciples, before his passion, from whence these expressions are taken, accumulates promise and prophecy together; and from the general substance of that affecting discourse, as far as it related to the mission and offices of the Holy Spirit, the following reflections seem to be justly drawn.

1. That Jesus, before his passion, as Lamb of God, perfectly knew and defined the

[e] John xvi. 14. [f] John xvi. 15.

office

office of the Spirit, as well as his own, in accomplishing the divine plan of human redemption; and accordingly predicted, that, in completion of the promise of the Father, and his own, the Holy Ghost would be sent by both, to [g] enable the disciples to perfect that divine purpose of Gospel-salvation, which he had already opened, and would enable them to carry on.

2. That the [h] counsel of peace was between the Father, and the Lamb of God; and that the respective offices of each, in the scheme of redemption, namely, the good-pleasure of the Father to accept, in behalf of man, that sacrifice of himself, which Christ, as Son of God, came down from heaven to offer, as well as the regular steps and order, in which that scheme would unfold itself, in all its parts, were as fully known to Jesus, as they were to the Father.

Thus far, with respect to the prophecy of the restoration of the Spirit, as it was delivered by Jesus, before his death, as Lamb of God. After his resurrection from the

---

[g] The Gospel is accordingly styled, " the ministration of the Spirit." 2 Cor. iii. 6, 8.
[h] Zechariah vi. 13.

dead,

dead, he thus repeated the prophecy; "¹ John truly baptized with water unto repentance, but ye shall be baptized with the Holy Ghost, not many days hence." This is an obvious repetition of that contrast, which John had formerly put, between the mission of the Spirit, and the baptism of water; and gives sufficient authority for considering the whole of the prediction, which Jesus gave, of the return of the Holy Spirit to the people of God, as parallel to the prophecy of John, " he shall baptize you with the Holy Ghost." In this passage, Jesus continues that particular style of expression, in which ᵏ he had usually delivered the same prophecy. The return of the Spirit had been characterized by the ancient prophets, and by the Baptist, under the symbol of water. It was therefore proper as well as striking, that he, by whose Spirit the prophets had foretold the return of the Holy Ghost, should, in delivering the same prediction, employ the prophetical style and language, especially when he was so soon to pour out the Spirit upon believers.

ⁱ Acts i. 5.
ᵏ John iv. 13. vii. 38. Compare Isaiah lviii. 7. Surenhus. Catallag. 358.

But,

But, although the expression of Christ, "ye shall be baptized with the Holy Ghost," was consonant to the language of John, and of the early prophets, yet his own prophecy was evidently original, since he enlarged the whole body of the prophecies, respecting the return of the Spirit, by the addition of new and important circumstances.

The limitations, as to time and place, were both original. — " Ye shall be baptized with the Holy Ghost, not many days hence," — "[l] tarry ye in the city of Jerusalem, until ye be indued with power from on high." In the last words of this command, another additional circumstance seems to be predicted. The [m] prophecy of Joel, to which saint Peter referred, as accomplished by the descent of the Holy Spirit, on the day of Pentecost, had not expressly mentioned, either the power of working miracles, or of speaking with other tongues, among the gifts of the Spirit. But Christ had already predicted, that both these powers should be conferred upon his disciples. [n] He that believeth on me, the works that I do, shall he do also,

---

[l] Luke xxiv. 49.
[m] Acts ii. 16. See Whitby, 1 John v. 6.
[n] John xiv. 12.

and

and greater works than these shall he do, because I go to my Father," — "° these signs shall follow them, that believe; in my name shall they cast out devils; they shall speak with ᵖ new tongues." He must therefore be understood to predict both these spiritual gifts, in the general prophecy of the mission of the Holy Ghost, as a Spirit of power; and thereby to have made a great addition to the parallel prediction of the Baptist, as well as to the ancient prophecies, of the return of the Spirit to Israel.

If then the several circumstances, related by saint Luke in the Acts, that the disciples were baptized with the Holy Ghost, according to the promise of Jesus, in the time, and at the place, which he had assigned, and, with fire, according to the prophecy of the Baptist, be taken together into consideration, the following conclusions seem to stand upon a fair foundation.

1. That, as John, in predicting the effusion of the Holy Ghost, with circumstances, before unrevealed, appeared an original pro-

---

° Mark xvi. 17.
ᵖ The Apostle refers to this power, as the testimony of Christ, 1 Cor. i. 5. ἐν παντὶ λόγῳ, in every tongue.

phet,

phet, so also Jesus necessarily stands in the same light, since he enlarged the prophecy of John, and expressly particularized, at what time, in what place, and with what miraculous powers, the Spirit would return.

2. That the effusion of the Spirit upon believers, either to consecrate them to the ministry, or to initiate them in the profession, of the Gospel, was as much ⁣ᵠ the personal act of Jesus, as baptizing the Messiah by water, to his prophetical office, had been the personal act of John.

Lastly, that the actual advent of the Spirit, according to the prophecy, and the promise, of Jesus, affords incontestable evidence, that he really ascended to the Father, "ʳ sat down on the right hand of the Majesty on high," and that all power was given unto him, in heaven and earth.

To proceed, — The conversion of the Gentiles, and their adoption to the inherit-

---

ᵠ The effusion of the Holy Ghost, is admitted to be one of the characteristics of the Messiah, by Abarb. on Isaiah xi. 2. See Rom. v. 15, 17. Gal. iv. 6. Eph iv. 7. Tillots. Serm. 144.

ʳ The Spirit is a witness to Christ 1 Cor. i. 5. Lightfoot, Hor. Heb. et Talm. Vol. ii. 740. 1 Tim. iii. 16. 1 John v. 6.

ˢ Heb. i. 3. viii. 1.

SERMON VII.

ance of that blessing, which had been originally promised to all families of the earth, through the Messiah, as the true ^t seed of Abraham, as it was a very important revolution in the spiritual state of mankind, was accordingly predicted, on many occasions, by the Son of God, to whom the ^u Father had promised the heathen for an inheritance, and the utmost parts of the earth for a possession.

It was formerly observed, that the caution, given by the Baptist to his audience, " think not to say within yourselves, we have Abraham to our father; for I say unto you, that God is able, of these stones, to raise up children unto Abraham," really predicted the rejection of Israel, and the adoption of the Gentiles to the inheritance of the patriarch's blessing, as fully and clearly, as that early and introductory state of the Gospel seemed to allow. That admonition of John may therefore be considered as prophetical, and parallel to all the

---

[t] Gal. iii. 16. " He saith not unto seeds, as of many, but as of one; and to thy seed, which is Christ." Seeds, must mean many, and not, one. —— Seed, may mean, one; (comp. Gen iv. 25.) and on that, as the true sense of it, the Apostle seems to insist.
[u] Psalm ii. 8.

prophecies, which Jesus delivered, of the call of the Gentiles, and the rejection of Israel.

The following prediction of Jesus is very similar to that prophetical admonition. "[w] Many shall come from the east, and from the west, and shall sit down with Abraham, Isaac and Jacob, in the kingdom of heaven; but the children of the kingdom shall be cast out into outer darkness." This language seems to have been designedly assimilated to the tenor of the promise, to Jacob. "[x] I am the Lord God of Abraham thy father, and the God of Isaac;— thy seed shall be as the dust of the earth, and thou shalt spread abroad to the west, and to the east, and to the north, and to the south; and in thee, and in thy seed, shall all the families of the earth be blessed." The Gospel was thus [y] preached to Jacob, as before to Isaac and Abraham; and for one and the same reason, that the admission of all families of [z] the earth, together with the patriarchs, into the kingdom of heaven, was foretold by Jesus;

---

[w] Mat. viii. 11.   [x] Genes. xxviii. 13, 14.
[y] See Galat. iii 8.   [z] Comp. Luke xiii. 29.

namely,

namely, because "God would justify the heathen through *a* faith." The children of the kingdom should alone be cast out; "*b* the kingdom of God shall be taken from you, and given to a nation, bringing forth the fruits thereof;" and with an immediate view to the conversion of the heathen, and the rejection of the Jews, Jesus seems elsewhere to speak, in very explicit terms; "other *c* sheep I have, which are not of this fold; them also I must bring, and they shall hear my voice."

These, and other similar declarations of Jesus, correspond, not only to the abovementioned prediction of the Baptist, but also, to many of the noblest prophecies in the old Testament. But, however consonant these predictions may seem to foregoing prophecy, they appear nevertheless not to have been derived from any divine revelation, that preceded the coming of Jesus, and therefore to ascertain his mission from God.

This may possibly be placed in a clearer

---

a Of which the Gentile Centurion gave so illustrious an example, that Christ took immediate occasion from it, to predict the adoption of all others, like him, to the inheritance of Abraham's blessing. Matth. viii. 11.
b Mat. xxi. 43. *c* John x. 6. See 1 Pet. ii. 25.

light, by comparing the conduct of Jesus, as a teacher of Israel, with his own prediction, as a prophet.

The mission of Christ was not of universal extent. "ᵈ I am not sent, he says, but unto the lost sheep of the house of Israel;" and the immediate benefits of his presence upon earth, were exclusively styled by himself, "ᵉ the children's bread." Conformably to this restriction in his own ministry, he ᶠ limited the first commission of the Twelve; "go ᵍ not into the way of the Gentiles, and into any city of the Samaritans, enter ye not; but go rather to the lost sheep of the house of Israel."

The limitation, with respect to his own mission, seems, at the first view, to contradict the declared purpose of his coming, "ʰ that the world through him might be saved;" and the interdiction, which he laid upon his Apostles, appears, at first sight, no less calculated to impede, rather than to

---

ᵈ Matth. xv. 24. Comp. Rom. xv. 8.
ᵉ Mark vii. 27.
ᶠ Hence, when the Greeks, John xii. 22, desired to see Jesus, Philip declined leading them to him, and consulted Andrew, whether he should do it. See Whitby ad l.
ᵍ Matth. x. 6.   ʰ John iii. 17.

promote, the accomplishment of the old-Testament prophecies, and his own.

A proper apprehension of the Gospel-scheme, and of the just dependency of its parts upon each other, will indeed render it easy to perceive, that these apparent inconsistencies are not real. But the question is not, whether they are real; but simply, whether the conduct of Christ, thus at once to predict the call of the Gentiles, and yet, at the same time, to delay the completion of it, and to undertake in his own person, and confer upon others, a limited commission, although he was an universal Saviour, could reasonably be ascribed to the prophecies, or to any known interpretation of them. According to all appearances, this conduct, in the Messiah, could not be explained or accounted for, by any Jewish construction of Scripture; and the prophetical writings, although sufficient evidences of the divine mission of Jesus, after his ministry had explained them, were nevertheless not distinct enough, to have afforded any adequate preconception, of the regular steps and method, by which he proceeded.

If then the conduct of Jesus, in the particulars abovementioned, be compared with ancient

ancient prophecy, and with his own, it will probably appear, that he acted under those views, and made that disposition of things, in his work of redemption, which divine revelations, previous to his coming, had never discernibly marked, and to which, of course, they did not lead. He came to fulfil all things, that were written of him; but some, as Lamb of God, and many more, as Son of God, and universal king. In these characters he discriminated, and referred to each the acts and predictions, severally appropriated to it. He applied himself, and sent his disciples, at first, to Israel only; for, since he had not been promised, as a teacher upon earth, to the world at large, he might, in that character, have one peculiar nation, for his immediate object; but, as his redemption was universal, his ultimate object, as a Saviour, must be all mankind. It was not his ministry, merely as a teacher upon earth, but the accomplishment of his character, as Lamb of God, that obtained the reconciliation of the world; and the Gentiles, who were afar off, were first to be made nigh by the blood of his cross, and his passion was

to

SERMON VII.

to [i] precede his glory in their admiſſion to his kingdom.

In this ſcheme of univerſal redemption, both the vengeance and mercy of God were conſpicuouſly diſplayed. It was a diſpenſation of the greateſt ſeverity to the peculiar people, who fell, and were rejected, through unbelief; but of infinite goodneſs to thoſe, who had been "ſtrangers to the covenants of promiſe," and were adopted through faith. "[k] Fill ye up then the meaſure of your fathers," was therefore an addreſs doubly prophetical. It implied that the Jews, after the example of their fathers, who had ſlain the prophets, would put Jeſus alſo to death; and that the caſting away of Iſrael, incurred thereby, would bring on the reconciliation of the world.

This was that myſtery of Chriſt, which, from the beginning of the world, had been hid in God. The great and univerſal bleſſings, that would enſue upon the complete revelation of it, were indeed magnificently diſplayed by the prophets; and they had deſcribed the office and dignity of the Meſ-

---

[i] Iſaiah liii. 10, 11, 18. Luke xiii. 2. Hebr. v. 9, 10. ſq.
[k] Matth. xxiii. 32.

L 4 ſiah,

fiah, and predicted his sufferings and glory. But the whole body of the prophecies dwelt upon the final issue and event of the scheme of redemption, rather than stated, the exact process, by which the Redeemer would conduct it, and the particular and material differences, in the state of his church, before and after his passion, which would regulate his proceedings and predictions.

Foregoing revelation therefore could not be the source, from whence he drew; the divine plan itself must have been his guide, in adjusting the order and arrangement of the constituent and intermediate parts, and gradually filling up the whole. A regular and expanding system had been settled in the divine mind; of which only some partial and indistinct views, though fully sufficient for the purposes intended, had been communicated to mankind. But Jesus distinguished the several means and parts from each other, and conducted their progress and gradual operation to the accomplishment of the divine mercies, in the appointed season. What the prophets had accumulated in general and indefinite terms, the course of his ministry drew out, and distributed in that regularity and order, in which the divine
mind

mind had previously disposed them. By
" the Spirit, which ˡ searcheth all things,
yea, the deep things of God," he knew
through what means, and at what time, the
counsel of the Father would be finally completed; and accordingly saw where to forbear, and what to prophecy, and how far to
limit or extend his views and operations.
He predicted the call of the Gentiles, because
it was in the divine intention; but he delayed
that call, because the peculiar church of the
Jews was not dissolved, and the preference of
Israel to the Gentiles still subsisted. But
when in the body of his flesh through death,
ᵐ he had presented the Gentiles, " holy and
unblameable, and unreproveable in the sight
of God," then the mediatorial kingdom was
begun; and then he delivered an unlimited
commission to his Apostles, " ⁿ all power is
given unto me, in heaven and in earth; go
ye therefore, and teach all nations." The
Jews had crucified the Lord of glory, and
thereby forfeited all privilege and preference
in the divine blessings. The distinction between Jew and Gentile immediately upon

---

ˡ 1 Cor. ii. 10.   ᵐ Coloss. i. 22.
ⁿ Math. xxviii. 18, 19.

this

this expired; and both were admitted by the Father, upon the same conditions of repentance and faith, into the fellowship of his Son, who was now the universal Prince and Saviour.

The body of the Jews, notwithstanding, rejected the Gospel-offer of salvation. The consequence of this aggravated insult to the mercy of God, is urged by the Apostles of the Gentiles; "° it was necessary that the word of God should first have been spoken to you, but seeing ye put it from you," ᵖ be it known therefore unto you, that the salvation of God is sent unto the Gentiles, and that they will hear it."

The expression of Jesus, " ᵍ let the children first be filled," was grounded upon his distinct foreknowledge of all these circumstances, with respect both to their progress and final effect in extending the blessing of Abraham to the Gentiles, and ʳ gathering them together with the Jews into one body, and giving access to both by ˢ one Spirit unto the Father.

° Acts xiii. 45.
ᵍ Mark vii. 27.
ˢ Ephes. ii. 18.
ᵖ xxviii. 23.
ʳ Gal. iii. 14.

In the great result of these circumstances, all successively tending to fulfil the salvation of the world, the riches of the divine mercy lay, undiscovered by all, except the Son of God, in whom were hid all the treasures of wisdom and knowledge. By his Spirit, as only-begotten of God, he entered into, and fully comprehended, the compass and depth of the counsel of peace between himself and the Father, and, being made in the likeness of man, directed and accomplished the scheme. ———

These reflections, which have arisen from a comparison of the conduct of Jesus, as a teacher upon earth, with his own prediction, as a prophet, have tended to shew, that his prophecy of the call of the Gentiles, had not been drawn from any foregoing revelation from God. Other circumstances also, which Jesus has added to the prophecy, have the same tendency to prove him a real and original prophet. Such are, the views, which he gave, of the prevalence of his Gospel, through the Roman empire, before the fall of Jerusalem; and of its extending to the four winds of heaven, before his last coming. But passing over these, I shall
mention

mention only one other evidence, that he acted by a real and personal foreknowledge.

This evidence seems to be contained in the words, "thou art [t] Peter, and upon this rock, I will build my church;" and I will give unto thee the keys of the kingdom of heaven."—The sequel of the passage extends to all the Twelve; but this extract seems exclusively restrained to Peter.

The import of the first clause, "thou art Peter, and upon this rock I will build my church," may perhaps be determined from other passages of Scripture. The faithful, which are styled God's [u] building and [w] the household of God, are said to be built upon the foundation of the Apostles and prophets; and the wall of the heavenly city is described, in the book of [x] Revelation, to have twelve foundations, and in them, "the names of the twelve Apostles of the Lamb." So that, apparently, in whatsoever sense the church would be founded upon Peter, in the same it would be built upon [y] all the Twelve.

[t] Matth. xvi. 18.   [u] 1 Cor. iii. 9.   [w] Eph. ii. 10.
[x] Rev. xxi. 14.   [y] Comp. Gal. ii. 9. James, Cephas, and John, who seemed to be pillars.

SERMON VII.

The meaning of the subsequent clause, seems also to be easily assignable. — The Pharisees are reproached for [a] shutting up the kingdom of heaven; and woe is denounced to the teachers of the law, for having taken away "the key of knowledge." By parity of expression, to lead men into the way of Christian salvation, would be properly called, to [b] open for them the kingdom of heaven, and give them the key of knowledge.

To be the rock of the church, and to have the [c] power of the keys, seem therefore the common attributes of the apostolical office; but the words of saint Peter, to the synod at Jerusalem, sufficiently imply the real difference, that subsisted between himself and his colleagues, in both these respects. "[d] Men and brethren, ye know how that a good while ago God made

---

[a] Mat. xxiii. 13. Luke xi. 52.

[b] Christ styles himself " the door," and the gates of the Church are described, when once open, as open for ever. Isaiah lx. 11. — To open the door, denotes preaching the Gospel. Is. xxvi. 2. Acts xiv. 27. 1 Cor. xvi. 9. 2 Cor. ii. 12. Coloss. iv. 3. Rev. iii. 8.

[c] Non malè forte hùc conferas antiquum ritum tradendi clavum juxta pugillares apud Hebræos in doctorum suorum promotione; quæ certè ad concessam docendi potestatem spectabat. Marckius in Exercit. 5. Comp. Matth. xxiii. 13. 1 Cor. iii. 5. iv. 1. 2 Cor. iv. 5. vi. 4.

[d] Acts xv. 7.

choice

choice [e] among us, that the Gentiles by my mouth should hear the word of the Gospel." He justifies his present forwardness in advising what conduct they should pursue toward the Gentiles, from the choice, which God had made of him, to take the lead in opening the Gospel to them; and it is generally conceived, that he alludes to these very words of Jesus.

According to this interpretation of the words of Jesus to the disciple Peter, they contain an original prophecy, that he should first open the door of faith to the Gentiles, and, so far, become exclusively the [f] foundation of the Gentile church, which Christ, the master-builder, would raise upon the common labours of the Twelve. And accordingly, Cornelius, who, with his family, formed the first-fruits of the Gentile church, was particularly directed by an Angel, to send for Peter; and that Apostle had already been instructed, by [g] immediate revelation from

---

[e] ἐν ἡμῖν, i. e. had preferred him to the rest. See Marckius, Exercit. 5.

[f] The foundation, as a part of the building, may be said to be first, even with respect to priority of time only. — The word θεμέλιον seems compounded in this sense by the Seventy. Esdras. vii. 9. —— Θεμελίωσι τὴν ἀνάβασιν τὴν ἀπὸ Βαβυλῶνος, he took the first step in ascending from Babylon.

[g] See Benson. Hist. of Plant. Christ. Vol. I. pag. 234.

his

his Lord, to comply with the requeſt of Cornelius.

Saint Peter apparently confiders this circumſtance in the light of a privilege, but it is propoſed here, ſimply, as original; and, as it made a part of the prophecy of Jeſus, reſpecting the eſtabliſhment of his church among the Gentiles, it affords an obvious proof, that preceding revelations from heaven were no guides to him, but that his own views extended alike to every the greateſt, as well as the [h] moſt minute, particular, in the counſel of God.

To proceed, — Beſides the attribute of reigning over the Gentiles, another prerogative of a kingly character, namely, that of diſpenſing reward and puniſhment, was prophetically aſcribed to the Meſſiah by the Baptiſt, and aſſumed by Jeſus himſelf. Two ſeveral exerciſes of that power are predicted by both; one, over Iſrael, the other, over the world.

1. That dreadful vengeance, which Jeſus

[k] The more minute ſome of theſe things are in themſelves, the greater is the evidence of divine foreknowledge in the prediction of them; becauſe the conformity between the prediction and the hiſtory, is ſo much the more circumſtantial. Maclaurin. on the Prophecies, pag. 63.

would

would inflict upon Israel, for shedding the blood of the prophets, and his own, is thus predicted by himself. ———— "He beheld the city and wept over it, saying, if thou hadst known, even thou, at least in this thy day, the things which belong to thy peace, but now they are hid from thine eyes;— for the days shall come upon thee, that thine enemies shall cast a trench about thee, and keep thee in on every side, and shall lay thee even with the ground, and thy children within thee, and they shall not leave in thee, one stone upon another, because thou knewest not the time of thy visitation."

This passage delivers, in a short but striking detail, what the Baptist referred to in summary terms, "now the axe is laid unto the root of the trees;" and if all the prophetical [i] parables and discourses of Jesus, which bore an evident relation to his approaching vengeance upon Israel, could be seen at one view, he would probably be found to have accumulated the several circumstances, which lay dispersed in the writings of preceding prophets.

[i] Mat. xxi. 33, 41. xxii. 2, 7. xxiii. 34, 35. Luke xix. 12.

SERMON VII.

But from the many original circumstances, which Jesus has interwoven with his prophecy of the destruction of Israel, it appears evident, that the divine purpose itself, and not barely antecedent revelation from God, was the source of his prophecy.

I offer only some few examples.

1. He limited the completion of his judicial vengeance upon Israel, to that generation, and to that period of time, in which the Gospel should have been preached throughout the Roman empire. When he informed his Apostles and followers, that their suffering and death should precede it, he [k] excepted the Evangelist John, and intimated that he should survive it. He had before extended the same prediction to others, " there be some standing here, which shall not taste of death, till they see the Son of man coming

---

[k] The words of Christ were considered as a prophecy by the disciples. The extent of it was prolonged by them to the consummation of all things; but the Evangelist himself overrules that construction, and limits the prophecy to the coming of Christ; and, as if to fix the sense, and shew the accomplishment of it, he subjoins, " this is that disciple, that testifieth of these things, &c." As he wrote most probably after the destruction of Jerusalem, he might, at the same time, record this prophecy, and attest its completion.

in his kingdom;" "this generation shall not pass, till all these things be fulfilled."

2. He not only particularized every bloody and ignominious circumstance, that would attend and follow the siege and downfal of Jerusalem, but also described the short and dreadful period, between the delivery and the accomplishment of his prediction, and gave a prophetical history of that interval. The people of Israel are represented as falling from deep to deeper wickedness and woe. The coming of false Messiahs, to deceive them; their slaughter of his Apostles and disciples; wars and bloodshed among nations and cities; hatred and treachery between [l] parents and children; famine, earthquake, pestilence; are all expressly enumerated, as signs that the utter ruin of Israel drew near. These are called, her "beginning of sorrows," ἀρχὴ ὠδίνων; what then were they to be, when her full time was come?

---

[l] Tacit. 15. (Whitby Mat. xxiv. 9, 10, 11.)— Joseph de B. Iud. l. 4. cap. 10. et 18. 1 Thess. ii. 4.

[m] On the approach of the legions to the city, those desperate bands, which had filled the whole country with slaughter, were driven within the walls. So that many, in Judæa and Galilee, escaped from their fury, by the siege being thus accelerated.

SERMON VII.

3. He prophetically promised, that they who, according to the call of the Baptist, and his own, had endeavoured to save themselves from this wrath to come, by faith in him, should then be the objects of divine protection. "For their sakes, these days of his vengeance should be ⁿ shortened;" and, with particular sollicitude for them, he pointed out the º standing of the Roman eagles in the holy place, as their appointed signal for immediate escape. However imminent the danger was, and however short the time, before the enemy returned; yet

---

celerated. —— Before the siege, they had destroyed their own resources of corn; and by intestine slaughter hastened and facilitated the triumph of their enemies. These were some of the causes, that enabled many, who had fled to the barren mountains of Peræa, and others, even in the city itself, to support themselves there, till the end of these tribulations.

ⁿ Matth. xxiv. 22.

º Mat. xxiv. 25. The Roman standard was ναὸς μικρὸς, κ̀ ἐν αὐτῷ ἀετὸς χρυσοῦς, a little shrine, with a golden eagle in it. (Dion. in Hamm. ad Mat. xxiv. 28.) Grotius shews from Arrian, Suetonius, Tacitus, Justin, and Tertullian, that the Roman standards exhibited the image of the Emperor, and were, on that account, adored by the Legions. —— an Idol is called an abomination. 1 Kings xi. 5, 7. 2 Kings xxiii. 13. Jerem. vii. 30. xxxii. 34. Ezek. vii. 20. The Roman Eagles appeared before the city, under Cestius Gallus; but suddenly disappeared, and erelong returned under Titus. In that interval, according to Josephus, many escaped; and according to Ecclesiastical writers, many Christians fled to Agrippa's dominions, in Peræa, and took shelter there.

the favourable moment might be, and was, seized with succefs, by all thofe, who believed in Chrift and his prophecy, and not in ᵖ falfe Chrifts, and falfe prophets, who would fay " peace and fafety, when fudden deftruction cometh upon them."

4. He predicted alfo the captivity of the Jews in all nations; and even the prefent ftate of Jerufalem, thus " trodden down of the Gentiles;" and limited the captivity of the one, and the defolation of the other, to that period, when the times of the Gentiles fhall be fulfilled. The prefent condition of the Jews, not only affords teftimony to the accomplifhment of this prophecy, in that part of it, which denounced the end of their ftate; but alfo gives the ftrongeft affurance of its future completion, in the remaining part, which feems to promife, that, " Jeru-

---

ᵖ The general character, which Jofephus applies to fome of them, βασιλείαν ὁ καιρὸς ἀνέπειθι, fhews the operation of principles, which the Gofpels afcribe to the Jews, viz. that the time of the Meffiah's appearance was confeffedly come, and that his leading object fhould be the temporal deliverance of Ifrael. The fame principles, that formed the ground of all thefe impoftures, would tend to produce their fuccefs. Jofephus adds, that thefe falfe Chrifts fhewed σημεῖα ϗ τέρατα; whence it is evident, that a miraculous power, was a credential of the true Meffiah, though Maimonides affirms the contrary.

salem shall cease to be trodden down of the Gentiles, and that Israel shall see Jesus coming to her in his mercy, as he came now in his wrath, when the times of the Gentiles shall be fulfilled, and the Jews shall be disposed to say, " blessed is he that cometh in the name of the Lord."

These are only some few [q] of the many original circumstances, with which Jesus enlarged the views, that foregoing prophets had given, of the destruction of Israel; but these seem sufficient to shew, that the divine mind, and not antecedent prophecy, had been the source, from whence he drew, and that all the purposes both of the vengeance and mercy of God were equally known to him.

The history of Josephus, a Jewish priest, and an eye-witness of the transactions, which he describes, yields at once a commentary, and a testimony, to this prophecy of Jesus; and the more closely the prediction and the detail of that historian are compared to-

---

[q] This capital prophecy has been frequently, and very distinctly, explained; the following are among those writers, who have already discussed it. Chandler, Diss. annexed to Comm. on Joel. Grotius and Whitby, on Matth. xxiv.—— Newton. Diss. on proph. Vol. ii. pag. 24. Jortin Rem. on Eccl. Hist. Vol. i. Tillotson's Sermon. 184. sq.

gether, the greater will be our astonishment, that the dire imprecation of the Jews, "his blood be on us, and on our children," should be so signally and literally fulfilled; and the prediction itself, in all its parts, if taken together with the accomplishment, affords the strongest evidence of the divine mission of Jesus, as a prophet; of his entire knowledge of the will and purposes of the Father, as Son of God; and of his judicial power, as a king.

2. This act of his regal authority over Israel, prefigures his final and universal judgment of the world; and as he came virtually or by his power, in this first exercise of his judgement, and will come really and in person, in the last, both of them are styled his coming, in his ' kingdom, in the clouds, and in his glory, and are called, the sign of the Son of man. Hence,

---

' The destruction of Israel seems to be called Christ's coming. John xxii. 21. —— In clouds, Revel. i. 7. this expression does not necessarily mean only a real and personal coming. comp. 2 Sam. xxii. 8. See Lightfoot and Whitby on Matth. xxiv. 31.——In glory with Angels, Mat. xxiv. 30.——It is styled Christ's inthroning, Matth. xix. 28. Luke xxii. 30. — See Lightfoot, Hor. H. et T. 461.

in the same capital prophecy, he seems to speak, in a primary sense, of his approaching judgement upon Israel, and in an ultimate sense, of his last judgement of the world. The same observation was formerly applied to the prophetical words of the Baptist; " whose fan is in his hand, and he will thoroughly purge his floor, and gather his wheat into the garner, but he will burn up the chaff with unquenchable fire." As the terms, here used, seem rather to denote a personal than a virtual parousia, the passage appears principally to respect the last coming of the Messiah to judge the world; and in that view is parallel to the following prophecies of Christ. " The Son of man shall come in his glory, and all the holy angels with him, then shall he sit upon the throne of his glory; and before him shall be gathered all nations, and he shall separate them one from another, as a shepherd divideth his sheep from the goats; and he shall set the sheep on his right hand, but the goats on his left. Then shall the king say unto them on his right hand, come, ye blessed of my Father, inherit the kingdom, prepared for you from the foundation of the *world. Then shall he say also unto them on the left hand, depart from me, ye cursed, into everlasting fire." " The Son of man shall come in the glory of the Father, with his angels, and then shall he reward every one according to his works." He predicted the vengeance, which he would inflict upon his enemies, and the safeguard, that he would afford to his elect, in this life; together with the endless misery, to which he will condemn the wicked, and the unspeakable happiness, to which he will receive the righteous, in another.

From the substance of this discourse it seems to be justly inferred; that the divine glory of the Spirit in Jesus, was signally displayed in his predictions, and promises, since he distinctly foresaw, as a prophet, and personally promised, as Son of God, all the means and operations either of grace or of vengeance, which were appointed to establish, to extend, to support, and to finish, his mediatorial kingdom;

⁵ Matth. xxv. 31.

and

and that, by the accomplishment of his prophecies and his promises, in many respects, he has given sufficient evidence that he is true and faithful, possessed of all knowledge, and of all power, both as the author and the finisher of our faith.

SERMON VIII.

JOHN xiii. 19.

Now I tell you before it come, that when it is come to pass, ye may believe that I am He.

THE prophecies of Jesus, which have been already considered, were parallel to predictions of John, and bore a direct relation, and, by their accomplishment, gave evident testimony, to the character of Jesus, as Son of God. In order to shew, that his prophecy of the establishment and prevalence of his kingdom in the world had the same respect, and by its completion gave the same attestation, to his character, as Son of God, I propose to consider that prophecy, in the present discourse.

The

The Messiah and his kingdom, are prophetically represented in the [a] old-Testament, as gradually advancing, from a small and obscure rise, to full size and brightness. The import of those predictions seems to be prophetically implied in the words of the Baptist, "he must increase;" and in many passages, parallel to this clause of John, Jesus foretold his own increase and the establishment of his kingdom, with circumstances, expressively denoting the unpromising beginning and final fulness of it. He compared it to a little leaven, by which the whole is leavened; and to [b] the least of all seeds, which, when it is grown, is the greatest among herbs, and becometh a tree; and when he encouraged the Apostles, as the intended stewards and rulers of his household, "[c] fear not, little flock, it is your Father's good pleasure to give you the kingdom," he seems to have spoken partly with a prophetical view to their future ministry of his Gospel.

---

[a] Psalm cxviii. 22. Isaiah xlix. 7. liii. 2, &c. Daniel ii. 34, 35.
[b] Matth. xiii. 32, 33.
[c] Luke xii. 32. compared with verse 41, 42.

Indeed,

Indeed, the prevalence of Christianity, considered as the accomplishment of the prophecy of Jesus, affords strong evidence of his divine character; but it becomes stronger, upon considering that the prevalence of his Gospel must be ascribed immediately to himself. In the first of these two lights, it displays the divine foreknowledge of its author, while he ministered upon earth; and in the last, it ascertains his divine power, while he reigneth in heaven.

I shall therefore endeavour to shew, that nothing but his own accomplishment of his promises adjusted the means of establishing his kingdom to the end proposed, and thereby ensured the completion of his prophecy.

1. With this view, it may be observed, that the Apostles of Jesus, at the time of his going away from them, understood not the spiritual character and universality of his kingdom; and were unprovided with [d] many principal

---

[d] Compare Matth. xxviii. 20, " teaching them to observe all things, whatsoever I have commanded you,"—with John xiv. 26, " he shall bring all things to your remembrance, whatsoever I have said unto you." If the Twelve were already

requisites, for the successful discharge of their office. This was plainly confessed by their Lord, before his death; "*e* I have yet many things to say unto you, but ye cannot bear them now." These things would most probably, at that time, either have clashed with their ruling prejudices, or quite have overpowered their strength of mind. Jesus then indeed assigned a future remedy for these deficiencies; but thereby implied that they would still subsist, until the remedy should be given; and accordingly they *f* appear to have subsisted, at the time of his ascension.

Again, — Although the mission of the Twelve was of universal extent, yet, as being all Galilæans, they were obviously unable to propose the Gospel, supposing that they had completely understood it, to any, but Jews, and not even to them, without very considerable disadvantage. Unskilled, as it seems, in the *g* original text, and even the *h* Greek version, of

ready able to teach whatsoever Christ had commanded, the Spirit was not wanted, to remind them of whatsoever he had said unto them.

e John xvi. 12. See Whitby ad l.
f Acts i. 7.
g See Lightfoot, Vol. i. 285.
h Which the Greek of the New-Testament much follows. Lightfoot, Miscell. Vol. i. 1005.

the

SERMON VIII.

the prophecies, they could not confirm the Chriſtian faith, by appealing to the Jewiſh Scriptures. The firſt of theſe impediments rendered them utterly unable to "diſciple all nations;" and the laſt greatly diſqualified them for preaching with ſucceſs,[i] even to their own.

2. It may be obſerved, that their Apoſtolical [k] warfare, indiſpenſably required far greater fortitude of mind, than previous appearances indicate that they naturally poſſeſſed. After having heard the doctrines, and ſeen the miracles of Jeſus, after having preached in the cities of Iſrael, they had all forſaken him, and Peter had thrice denied him.

Beſides; their natural fears would be extremely aggravated, by the expreſs prophecy of Jeſus; "[l] behold I ſend you forth, as lambs among wolves;" "[m] ye ſhall be hated of all men for my name's ſake;" "[n] they ſhall deliver you up to be afflicted, and ſhall

---

[i] To Jews, the argument from the prophecy, would be particularly awakening. Hence, in their addreſſes to their countrymen, the Apoſtles commonly uſed it.
[k] 1 Tim. i. 18.
[l] Luke x. 3.
[m] Mat. x. 22. Luke xxiv. 9.
[n] Mat. x. 17.

kill

kill you." That part of the prediction, which related to saint Peter singly, was thus explained to him; "°when thou wast young, thou girdedst thyself, and walkedst whither thou wouldest; but when thou shalt be old, thou shalt stretch forth thy hands, and another shall gird thee, and carry thee whither thou wouldest not; this he spake, signifying by what death he should glorify God;" and it is generally understood to ᴾ imply crucifixion. The feelings and wishes of the Twelve would greatly add to the distresful effect of this prediction upon them. Full of hope to enjoy the glory of this world, in the kingdom of their Lord, they were not likely to receive his prophecy of their sufferings and ᑫ violent death, without extreme disappointment, aggravated by the utmost terror. And hence it may be observed, that if Jesus should

---

° John xiv. 36. xxi. 18.

ᴾ See Grot. et Wolf ad John xxi. 18. Petrus ab altero cingitur, cum cruci adstringitur. Tertull. Scorpiaco. The use of his hands, and of his feet, should be taken from him. This would not characterize any other death, but that of Crucifixion; and it is elsewhere characterized particularly by the suffering of the hands, and the feet; " they pierced my hands, and my feet," Psalm xxii. 16. The Apostle himself seems to allude to this prophecy of his Lord, 2 Pet. i. 13, 14, and it was accomplished soon after, in the persecution raised by Nero.

ᑫ Matth. xxiv. 9. Mar. xiii. 9. Luke xxi. 12, 16.

be supposed the author of imposture, his conduct in ruining the favourite hope of his adherents, even before they understood that faith, which he designed them to propagate, and in shewing them a world, prepared to persecute and destroy them ʳ for his name's sake, as it would certainly tend to frustrate his own design, seems entirely irreconcilable with every known principle of nature. There were no assignable means of overcoming the natural effect of his prediction upon them, except a commanding sense of duty, founded upon the real truth of the Gospel, and animated by the promise of its author to support them. Besides, his direction to the disciples not to ˢ meditate before what they should answer, still further aggravated the case. He gave them a foresight of danger, yet forbad them to prepare defence; and apparently abandoned them to that persecution, under which he taught them, at the same time, they would assuredly sink.

ʳ Hence Tertullian calls the persecution of the Christians, "nominis prælium." See Newton on Prophecies. Vol. ii. pag. 253.
ˢ Luke xxi. 14.

According to this representation, Jesus left his Apostles without that knowledge of his Gospel, which their office necessarily required; and, if they had really understood it, without the power of proposing it, to any but Jews, although they were sent to people of all tongues; and not even to Jews, without great disadvantage; and besides, without fortitude, equal to the undertaking. No adequate causes of the accomplishment of the prophecies, that Jesus must increase, and the kingdom be given to his little flock, seem therefore to have existed, at the time of his ascension.

Yet if, as [t] saint Luke certifies, the Apostles actually entered upon the ministry of the Gospel, not many days after the departure of their Master, one of the two following points will be necessarily true; either, that they exercised their office under such signal deficiencies, or that these impediments were previously removed by the power of their Lord, according to his promise.

---

[t] Acts ii. 14. That the book of the Acts of the Apostles, was written by St. Luke, and contains a true history, hath been shewn from various external and internal testimonies, by Benson, in a particular dissertation, at the end of Hist. of the first planting of the Christian religion, Vol. ii. pag. 318.

The first of these cases scarcely seems defensible; for then the fact would be, that a system of Gospel-faith was, at first, clearly proposed by persons, who did not themselves justly comprehend it; and the most implacable persecution, and even the utmost bitterness of death, voluntarily incurred by men, who were naturally disposed to shrink at a much less formidable danger.

This difficulty can be avoided only by supposing, that their deficiencies were actually remedied, before the commencement of their ministry. But the interval, between the ascension of Jesus and their publication of his Gospel, was of inconsiderable length; and the first view, which they gave of it, was comprehensive and clear, and, besides, was proposed with fervency, and " " much assurance." An improvement so great and sudden, both in their views of the Christian scheme, and in their strength of mind, can not reasonably be ascribed to their natural powers.

According to appearances then, the increase of Jesus and of his kingdom, foretold by the Baptist and himself, could not be

" 1 Thess. i. 5.

provided for without his accomplishment of that prophecy, which he had delivered, in his last words to the disciples; "ye shall [w] receive power, after that the Holy Ghost is come upon you." He had before predicted the advent, and had promised the mission, of another divine agent in the work of redemption, and had directed the Apostles to [x] wait at Jerusalem for his coming, as it was his distinct and proper office to remove those very incapacities, under which they laboured. "Behold, I send the promise of my Father upon you;" "when he, the Spirit of truth, is come, he will guide you into all truth;" he shall teach you all things, and bring all things to your remembrance, whatsoever I have said unto you."

Jesus by actually fulfilling this prophecy and promise baptized them with the Holy Ghost; and having himself the Spirit without measure, he gave unto them [y] of his own fulness. The Holy Ghost, when he de-

---

[w] Summam hic proponit tot sermonum Apostolicorum, quos hic liber (Act. Apost.) exhibebit. Confer Marc. xvi. 20. Grot. ad Acts i. 7.

[x] Acts i. 4.

[y] John i. 16. Eph. ix. 13.

scended, accomplished ᶻ his offices of advocate and witness to Jesus, by his influence upon the Apostles, as a Spirit of truth, and a Spirit of power; and the evidence of his actual coming upon them immediately and publickly appeared.

Indued by him, as a Spirit of truth, with "ᵃ the word of wisdom," and enriched by him, as a Spirit of power, with " all utterance," the Apostles were at once enabled to communicate to men of every tongue all the doctrines which Jesus had already delivered, and whatever else came to them then or afterwards by revelation from God.

ᶻ John xvi. 13. ἐκεῖνος τὸ Πνεῦμα, he, that Spirit of truth. Clarke, Scrip. Doct of the Trinity, p. 202. comp. Eph. i. 13, 14. " that holy Spirit of promise, which (ὅς, who) is the earnest, &c.

ᵃ i. e. a comprehensive view of the doctrines and mysteries of the Christian religion. See 1 Cor. i. 24. ii. 6. Ephes. i. 17. St. Paul is said by St. Peter, (2 Ep. iii. 15.) to have written his epistles, according to " the wisdom given unto him." In the catalogue of spiritual gifts, 1 Cor. xii. 8, the " word of wisdom" stands first; and in the list of those, who received the several gifts of the Spirit, the Apostles are placed first, (28, 29.) so that the Apostles only seem to have received the " word of wisdom," that is, were enabled to speak by revelation, 1 Cor. xiv. 6. Superior prophets and evangelists, learned from the Apostles, 2 Tim. i. 2, what they learned from immediate revelation. Thus also the Apostle Paul received not the Gospel from man, but immediately from Jesus Christ. 1 Cor. xv. 3. Galat. i. 11, 12, 19.—See Benson, Hist. of planting. C. R. Vol. i. pag. 40, 41. and the note at pag. 182.

Renewed by him, as a Spirit of power, in the temper of their minds, out of weakness they were made strong, from being fearful they waxed bold, and continued to the end exactly the reverse of what they had been in the beginning. That Peter, in particular, could maintain the exercise of his ministry through a life of continual hardship and struggle, under the certainty of ending it, like his Lord, upon the cross, he owed to the [b] former intercession of Jesus, that his faith might not fail; and to this accomplishment of his promise, which enabled him to speak " [c] the word of God with boldness."

Invested, besides, with a miraculous power of the largest extent, they " came behind in no gift;" but, more highly favoured than former prophets, and, in some degree, resembling their Lord himself, they uniformly displayed the fullest criteria of a divine mission, the exercise of spiritual gifts, in their own persons, and [d] the communication of them unto others, [e] discerning of spirits, prophecy, and miracles.

[b] Luke xxii. 31.
[c] Acts iv. 31.
[d] Acts viii. 14.
[e] Acts v. 3, 9. viii. 21, 23. xiii. 10. xiv. 9.

Their manifold incapacities for preaching the Gospel would therefore, as it seems, unavoidably have remained in all their former force, if Jesus had not sent to them, according to his promise, "the Spirit of truth, which is the Holy Ghost." He it was, who ᶠ brought the Gospel down from heaven, and shined in their hearts, to give "ᵍ the light of the knowledge of the glory of God, in the face of Jesus Christ." As they were but "earthen vessels," unfit for the spiritual use, to which they were appointed; the excellency of the power, which was treasured up in them, the more plainly appeared to be of God.

But even after this effusion of the Spirit upon them, they were still permitted to remain ʰ unacquainted with the principle, upon which salvation would be extended to the Gentiles; so that, even in this capital point, they could not proceed to the extent of their commission, without farther illumination. Jesus therefore personally instructed saint Peter, in the case of the Gentile

---

ᶠ 1 Thess. i. 5. 1 Cor. ii. 7, 10. 1 Pet. i. 12.
ᵍ 2 Cor. iv. 6. vii. 8.
ʰ See Grot. ad Act Apostol. ii. 39. ———— Benson Hist. of planting the C. R. Vol. ii. pag. 230.

Cornelius. Hence, and from many similar instances, it appears, that as the Twelve could not have opened their ministry, without an effusion of the divine Spirit upon them, so neither could they have proceeded in the discharge of it, without repeated inspiration from God.

II. The continuance of the law, was another great impediment to the increase of Jesus, and to the growth of his kingdom. Two divine dispensations subsisted at once in rivalship to each other. From this competition the minds of the Jews took different turns, but all unfavourable to the Gospel. Exclusive zeal for the law [i] exasperated the greater part of that people against Christianity, and particularly against those, who taught it. [k] All their craft, all their

---

[i] This was the chief ground of that opposition to the Apostles, which their contemporary Cerinthus gave. See Epiphanius, quoted by Whitby, ad Coloss. ii. 10. and Constit. Apostol. Lib vi. 10.

[k] 1. By an established prayer against Christians.——2. By emissaries, to decry the Gospel every where. Acts xix. 13. See Lightfoot on Acts, 289.——Of Jewish opposition to the Apostles, see Acts xiii. 45. xvii. 5. Rom. xv. 31. 1 Thess. ii. 14.—— James suffered at Jerusalem. Acts xii. 2. Joseph. Antiq. l. 20. Cap. 8. —— Antipas at Pergamus, Revel. ii. 12, 13. —— Peter at Babylon. Lightfoot, Hor. Heb. et Talm. 241.

power,

power, were exerted to check and overthrow it. They shed the blood of the Apostles and converts of Jesus, not perceiving, in the meanwhile, that they added to the evidence of his divine mission, by thus accomplishing his prophecies. Others of that nation yielded indeed, at first, to the evidence of the **Gospel, but without** any relaxation of their zeal for the law. They subverted **the** fundamental principle of Christianity, by associating Judaism with it, and obstinately ¹ shutting the door of faith **against** the Gentiles. Others of them, **who embraced** the Gospel, and submitted so far to the spirit of it, as not utterly to decline **communion** with the Gentiles, yet rigorously contended for imposing the yoke of the law upon them, and, probably when **the Apostolical council** at Jerusalem decided against them, renounced **the faith of Christ**, and ᵐ fell **back to the law.** ⁿ All these pursued their seve-

---

¹ Acts xi. 3. xv. 1, &c.

ᵐ Of the apostacy of many, See 2 Thess. ii. 3. Gal. iii. 2. 2 Tim. i. 15. Comp. Matth. xxiv. 12.

ⁿ In the Acts, and in the Epistles, especially those of saint Paul, many evidences occur, that these several principles prevailed among the Jews. See Acts xxi. 21. Rom. ii. 17. ——See Gal. ii. 4. and Whitby on Gal. iii. 4. and on James i. 19.

ral

ral principles, with bitter hostility to the true disciples of Jesus, and virtually laboured to subvert his kingdom. Every effort of Apostolical vigilance and industry, and all the authority of an Apostolical synod, would certainly have failed in supporting the little flock of Christ, against this weight of unrelenting and sanguinary opposition, if it had not been the Father's **good pleasure to give them the kingdom.**

The removal of this great obstacle to the increase of Jesus, and of his kingdom, depended upon his accomplishment of that woe, which he had denounced against the city, temple, and people of Israel, representing the shaking and downfal of their state, by the ᵒ convulsion and ruin of nature. By this signal act of his judicial authority, he had promised to ᵖ come and relieve his church, and to make a way for his own kingdom. Hence it seems frequently represented in the ᑫ Apostolical

---

ᵒ Comp. Isaiah xiii. 10. Ezek. xxxii. 7, 8. Joel. ii. 31. iii. 15.
ᵖ John xxi. 22.
ᑫ 1 Pet. iv. 7. Phil. iv. 5. 1 Thess. v. 2. Heb. x. 25. James v. 9.

Epistles,

Epistles, as the signal test, by which the true servants and the real kingdom of Jesus might be known, and by which the contest, between the two rival dispensations by Moses and himself, would be determined in favour of his own. As this prophecy was generally dispersed throughout the Roman empire, before the fall of Jerusalem, the minds of men were awakened to expect the accomplishment of it, as an eventual testimony for or against Jesus, and his Gospel.

That the prophecy was literally accomplished in the fall of the city, a short but striking evidence is given in the complaint of the Jew Eleazar, " [r] where is that city, whose inmate, as we believed, was God? From the foundations it is rooted up; and one only monument of it is left, the camp of those who destroyed it, still pitched on its remains."

An overthrow, no less complete, befel the Temple. What the lingering flames, though madly hastened by the Jews them-

---

[r] Joseph. de bell. Iud. Lib. vii. cap. 8. Ed. Hudf. See Newton, on Proph. Vol. ii. pag. 315.

selves, had left undone, the Roman ˢ ploughshare accomplished; it profaned and utterly defaced the holy place. The ᵗ sacred vessels were deposited in the temple of peace at Rome, and ᵘ the tribute, usually paid by the Jews to the God of Israel, was transferred to Jupiter of the Capitol, to whom erelong a temple was erected, ʷ on or near the site of the house of Jehovah.

These were indeed the days of wrath upon this people, and all things that were written against them were accomplished. They were thrown out, as a carcase, and the eagles were gathered together to devour it. The slain were innumerable; and they who survived, were either sold to slavery, or ˣ devoted to the sanguinary combats of the theatre, or reserved for the triumph of the

---

ˢ See Lightfoot, Whitby, and Wetstein. on Luke xix. 44.

ᵗ Joseph. de bell. Iud. Lib. vii. 24.

ᵘ Joseph. Lib. vii. cap. 27. φόρον δὲ, ὁπουδήποτ᾽ ἔσιν Ἰουδαίοις ἐπέβαλε δύο δραχμὰς, ἕκαστον κελεύσας ἀνὰ πᾶν ἔτος εἰς τὸ Καπετώλιον φέρειν, ὥσπερ πρότερον εἰς τὸν ἐν Ἱεροσολύμοις νεὼν συνετέλουν.—Xiphilin. ad Dion. Cass. Lib. 66. init. Καὶ ἀπ᾽ ἐκείνου δίδραχμον ἐτάχθη τοὺς τὰ πάτρια αὐτῶν ἔθη περιστέλλοντας τῷ Διὶ κατ᾽ ἔτος ἀποφέρειν.

ʷ Dion. Cass. Hist. Lib. lxix. p. 793. Ed. Leunclav. Hanov. 1606. Newton. on Proph. Vol. ii. pag. 317.

ˣ Josephus. de bell. Iud. Lib. vi. 9. §. ii. 3. et Lib. vii. Cap. ii. §. 1. Ibid.

con-

conqueror, in which ʸ the law of the Jews closed the train. From that time to this, their calamities have exceeded any that ever befel them, as a nation, before. They were together in Goshen, together in Babylon; Moses, was sent to them, and Ezekiel and Daniel prophesied, under their captivity. But they are separated now, and destitute of all divine communication, and entirely disabled from any further observance of their ceremonial worship, ᶻ consistently with the laws of that dispensation, to which they resolutely adhere. They seem to be ᵃ held up to the eyes of all nations, as a signal monument of the vengeance of Jesus now, as we hope they are reserved for the final display of his mercy.

This coming of Jesus, in his kingdom, to fulfil his own denuntiation of woe to the temple, the city, and people of Israel, broke the power of the Jews, and relieved his little flock; and thereby he subverted

---

ʸ Ὅτι νέμ[ε]σθ᾽ ὁ τῶν Ἰȣδαίων ἐπὶ τούτοις ἐφίετο, ᾧ λαφύρων τελȣ-ταῖ[ον]. Joseph. ibid. cap. 24.

ᶻ Deuteron. xii. 11, 12, 13, 14. 2 Kings viii. 29. 2 Chron. vii. 2.

ᵃ See Amos ix. 9. I will sift the house of Israel among all nations, like as corn is sifted in a sieve, yet shall not the least grain fall upon the earth.

the

the law, and left his Gospel to stand without a competitor, as a divine dispensation. This great event was a testimony to all men, that the peculiar church of Israel was dissolved, and that the spiritual kingdom of Jesus would comprehend all kindreds, and nations, and tongues. And accordingly, Jesus prophetically marked this act of his judicial power, as immediately and effectually leading to the universal establishment of his own kingdom; " he shall send [b] his angels, with a great sound of a trumpet, and they shall gather together his elect from the four winds." The trumpet of the Gospel would then be sounded, by the [c] messengers of Jesus, in all lands, and his elect should hear it, and be gathered unto him from one end of heaven to the other.

The Jews endeavoured, under Hadrian, to recover the remains of their city, with an intent to rebuild it, and restore the laws and worship of their fathers. In vain; they were [d] again given up to slaughter, and

---

[b] See Lightfoot, and Whitby, on this place.

[c] Ἄγγελος frequently means, simply, a messenger. Matth. xi. 10. Luke vii. 27. ix. 52. James ii. 25. Rev. ii. 1. See Olearii. Analyf. ep. ad Heb. pag. 11.

[d] See Eusebius, Jerome, Chrysostom, and Appian who lived at that time. Mede's Works, b. 3. pag. 443. all quoted by Newton. on proph. Vol. ii. 318, &c.

famine,

famine, and pestilence, and fire. — If any survived this second overthrow, them the edict of ᵉ Hadrian prohibited, ᶠ on pain of death, from entering, and even from beholding afar off, the miserable ruins of their city.

Another attempt was afterwards made by the emperor Julian, to defeat the accomplishment of this prophecy of Jesus, and to restore the law, as a rival to the Gospel, by rebuilding the temple, and recalling the dispersed people, of Jerusalem. But, without ᵍ minutely discussing the plain evidence of divine interposition, to prevent the execution of this design, it may perhaps be sufficient here to observe, that the prophecy and the promise of Jesus are not defeated of their accomplishment. The temple and city of Jerusalem continue " trodden down of the Gentiles," and the law is in no condition to contend, as a competitor, with the Gospel.

III. Another great obstacle to the increase of Jesus, and to the success of his little

---

ᵉ Euseb. H. E. Lightfoot. Vol. i. 367. Whitby. See Pref.
ᶠ See Lightfoot. Vol. i. pag. 367.
ᵍ See Whitby, Gen. Pref. pag. 28.——Lightfoot. Vol. i. 362.

flock in establishing his kingdom, is described in the words of the Apostle Paul; "[h] we wrestle not against flesh and blood, but against principalities, against powers, against the rulers of the darkness of this world, and against spiritual wickedness in [i] high places." This is a full description of what Scripture elsewhere compendiously calls the "power of darkness," and the kingdom of Satan, antagonist to the kingdom of God's dear Son. That enemy is the God of this world, the father of every thing that maketh a lie, and especially of religious abominations; using, in every age, and with all his power and subtlety, the false theology, the vain philosophy, and the

---

[h] Eph. vi. 12.

[i] ἐν τοῖς ἐπουρανίοις — scil. χρήμασι, says, Wolf. ad l. "in heavenly things, i. e. remission of sins, justification, adoption, &c. Chrysost. τὸ γὰρ ἐν τοῖς ἐπουρανίοις, ἀντὶ τοῦ, ὑπὲρ τῶν ἐπουρανίων, ἐςίν. —— But τόποις, is generally, and more probably, supplied. See Hamm. ad l. Satan is called in Scripture, "the Prince of the power of the air."—— He, and his confederacy,

—————— rul'd the middle Air,
Their highest Heaven. ——

Milton, P. L. i. 516.

The seventh phial, Rev. xvi. 17. is poured upon the Air, when idolatrous Babylon falls, which is styled (xviii. 2.) φυλακὴ παντὸς πνεύματος ἀκαθάρτου, and at whose fall "the holy apostles and prophets," (20) are called upon to rejoice.

corrupt

corrupt paffions of men, to fuftain his own kingdom, and to bear down that of God. He had his eftablifhment among the heathen nations, and his ᵏ fynagogue among the Jews, and " now worketh in the children of difobedience," and " blindeth their eyes, left the light of the glorious Gofpel of Chrift, who is the image of God, fhould fhine unto them."

To the whole power and confederacy of fuch a formidable enemy, affuming all fhapes, even that of an angel of light, the kingdom of Jefus is oppofed; and, having himfelf forefeen the conflict between them, he prepared his difciples for it, by giving them power, and promifing them fupport from himfelf; " behold," he faid to the feventy difciples," " I give unto you power to tread ˡ on ferpents and fcorpions, and over all the power of the enemy;" and to an Apoftle, " thou art Peter, and upon this rock will I build my church, and the gates of hell fhall not prevail againft it;" and,

---

ᵏ See 2 Cor. xi. 14. Rev. ii. 9, 10.

ˡ Luke x. 19. Ἵνα μὴ τὰ ἑρπετὰ ἀπολάβῃς, ἐπήγαγεν, " ὁ ἐπὶ πᾶσαν τὴν δύναμιν τοῦ ἐχθροῦ." δράκων ὁ ὄφις ὁ Διάβολος. Ex Photii Amphiloch. apud Wolf. Cur. Phil. Vol. v. ad calc. pag. 815.

to the disciples at large, after his resurrection, "lo, I am with you alway, even unto the end of the world."

Thus were the Apostles of Jesus prepared to encounter the ministers of Satan, and the Gospel was thus enabled to prevail over Heathenism, however recommended by Antiquity, or sustained by Civil Power. The uninterrupted completion of these promises of Jesus could alone ensure his encrease, and, in the midst of continual struggles, maintain the kingdom to his little flock; and the power of his disciples, through the Spirit, with which they were baptized, to discern this adversary, and to disarm and overcome him, was granted by Jesus himself, [m] who wrought with them, and " went forth conquering and to conquer," until the repeated shocks, which he gives to the kingdom of Satan, shall gradually have accomplished its downfal.

From the whole of this discourse it seems reasonable to infer; first, that, as Jesus left the Apostles, at his departure, destitute of the principal qualifications for the

[m] Comp. Gal. iv. 14.

ministry

ministry of the Gospel, his prophecy, that the good pleasure of the Father would give the kingdom to his little flock, was left by himself to depend entirely, for its accomplishment, upon his promised mission of the Spirit of the Father and the Son, to confer upon the Twelve that knowledge and power, which, although absolutely necessary for their success, were yet entirely unattainable by themselves. It was the test of his character, both as a prophet, and as Son of God; and, by the accomplishment of it, " him hath God the Father sealed."

2. That, as the peculiar kingdom of the Father over Israel still subsisted, and would stand in the way of his own universal one, Jesus, by subverting that kingdom, within the time and with the signal circumstances, foretold by himself, has evidently shewn that his increase, and the principles and establishment of his own kingdom, entirely coincided with the counsel and good pleasure of the Father.

3. That, as the power of the evil Spirit was and would be every where, and by every means, concealed or open, at all times

times exerted to lessen Jesus and his kingdom, he undertook to be present with believers by his power and his ⁿ grace, and to shew himself, alway even unto the end, °greater in them, than he that is in the world. And as the history of the church and of mankind concur to shew, that he has signally fulfilled and is now fulfilling his promise, he hath thereby given and still gives sufficient assurance, that he will proceed in maintaining the conflict, till Satan, as lightning, shall fall from heaven. —

Having now filled up the design, at first proposed, it remains only for me to state the general conclusions, which seem to result from the whole, that has been offered in these discourses.

The baptismal doctrine of John, and the ancient prophecies, respecting the Messiah and his kingdom, agreed in their true principles and import, and therefore might both proceed from the same divine Spirit. And, as the Baptist, in assigning the attributes of the Messiah, and characterizing his kingdom, proceeded upon the spiritual sense of Scripture, contrary to the notions and traditions

ⁿ Ephes. iv. 7. 1 John ii. 20. ° John iv. 4.

of the Jews; and, above all, added to the prophecies many new and original circumstances, which were afterwards fulfilled, it appears, that a divine revelation had been actually vouchsafed to himself.

Several attributes of the Messiah's person and office John, as his forerunner, predicted, before he knew him; and after the Messiah was personally notified to him by divine revelation, he ascribed to him many new characters, denoting his official and personal glory, which seemed not to have been revealed to the Baptist, at his original mission. These and other evidences were pointed out in proof that he acted under continual inspiration from God. All these characters John, as a witness, applied to Jesus of Nazareth, whom he had baptized to the office of Messiah. In order to shew that this application was just, he instanced the descent and abode of the Spirit upon Jesus, which he saw, and the voice of the Father, that proclaimed him his beloved Son, which he heard.

When Jesus entered upon his ministry, he assumed, and, by displaying the mighty works of the Father and of the Spirit, that dwelt in him, justified himself in assuming, the several characters, previously ascribed to him

him by the Baptift. At the same time he gave prophetical views of the various circumstances and situations, through which he should pass, and of several successive acts of power, which he would display, in accomplishing each of those characters, which the Baptift had ascribed to him, and which he had thus assumed to himself.

He also delivered prophecies, parallel indeed to those of John, but far exceeding the measure of the prophetical spirit in the Baptift. In his minute particularity, as to circumstances; in his exact limitations, as to time; and, in his original disposition and arrangement of things in the work of redemption, all implying the same perfect knowledge of the human and divine mind, the glory of the Spirit of God appeared through the veil of his flesh. And moreover, by promising to fulfil his own prophecies, and actually fulfilling them, after his death and resurrection, and after his ascending up, where he was before, to the glory, which he had with the Father, before the world was; in a word, by delivering prophecies and promises in his state of humiliation, which he has, to this time, signally accomplished in his state of glory, he

has

has given evidence, which strengthens daily, that he was the Son of God, and came down from heaven, and, being made perfect, in all his offices, is become the author of eternal salvation to them, that obey him.

The general substance of the foregoing discourses will, it is presumed, yield a sufficient foundation for these conclusions, if the authenticity of the Gospel-history, to which the appeal has all along been unreservedly made, cannot reasonably be disputed. With respect to this point, it may be urged, that many prophecies of Jesus, which have been already mentioned, namely, that his Gospel should be preached throughout the Roman empire, and most of his Apostles be put to death, and Peter particularly by crucifixion, before the end of Israel should come; and, that the city and temple of Jerusalem should be overthrown, and trodden down of the Gentiles, till the end of a period, not yet fulfilled; and that the Jews should " be carried captive into all lands," before that very generation of men should pass away; were all extant in written Gospels, long [n] before either

---

[n] The Gospel of St. Matthew is generally said to have been written in the eighth year after the ascension of Jesus; those of Mark and Luke, before the fall of Jerusalem. See this point pursued, and proved, at large, in Jortin's Rem. on Ecclef. Hist. Vol, i. pag. 41, &c.

of the predictions were accomplished. History, sacred, ecclesiastical, and profane, and even the present condition of Jerusalem and of the Jewish people, concur in their testimony, that all these prophecies either have been exactly fulfilled already, or are now in a course of accomplishment.

Since then the divine Spirit only, which foreseeth all things, could have dictated these prophecies, and the divine power only, which ordereth all things, could have exactly adjusted the several events to the predictions, as they stood in the New-Testament-writings; it seems evident that both at the first preaching of the Gospel by Jesus, and at the written publication of it by the Evangelists, God set his seal upon it, and marked it for his own, by applying his transcendent attributes of Prescience and Power, to witness and support it; and, consequently, that the baptismal predictions and testimony of John, and the prophecies of Jesus, as both are represented in the Gospels, were truly the witness of God, which he hath testified of his Son.

THE END.

www.ingramcontent.com/pod-product-compliance
Lightning Source LLC
Chambersburg PA
CBHW021819230426
43669CB00008B/808